P9-ASJ-362

LOW-FAT
TOP
SECRET
RECIPES

Creating Kitchen Clones of America's Favorite Brand-Name Foods

Todd Wilbur

With Illustrations by the Author

A PLUME BOOK

This book was not prepared, approved, licensed, or endorsed by any of the owners of the trademarks or brand names referred to in the book. Terms mentioned that are known or believed to be trademarks or service marks have been indicated as such. See section on "Trademarks."

PLUME
Published by the Penguin Group
Penguin Putnam Inc., 375 Hudson Street, New York, New York 10014, U.S.A.
Penguin Books Ltd, 27 Wrights Lane, London W8 5TZ, England
Penguin Books Australia Ltd, Ringwood, Victoria, Australia
Penguin Books Canada Ltd, 10 Alcorn Avenue, Toronto, Ontario, Canada M4V 3B2
Penguin Books (N.Z.) Ltd, 182–190 Wairau Road, Auckland 10, New Zealand

Penguin Books Ltd, Registered Offices: Harmondsworth, Middlesex, England

First published by Plume, a member of Penguin Putnam Inc.

Copyright © Todd Wilbur, 2000
All rights reserved

To the best of the author's knowledge, the information regarding company backgrounds and product histories is true and accurate. Any misrepresentation of factual material is completely unintentional.

 REGISTERED TRADEMARK—MARCA REGISTRADA

Printed in the United States of America

Without limiting the rights under copyright reserved above, no part of this publication may be reproduced, stored in or introduced into a retrieval system, or transmitted, in any form, or by any means (electronic, mechanical, photocopying, recording, or otherwise), without the prior written permission of both the copyright owner and the above publisher of this book.

ISBN 0-7394-1034-2

ACCLAIM FOR TODD WILBUR'S
TOP SECRET RECIPES SERIES

"There's something almost magically compelling about the idea of
making such foods at home . . . The allure is undeniable,
and [the books are] stuffed with tidbits and lore
you're unlikely to find anywhere else."
—*Boston Herald*

"The mission: Decode the secret recipes for America's favorite
junk foods. Equipment: Standard kitchen appliances.
Goal: Leak the results to a ravenous public."
—*USA Today*

"This is the cookbook to satisfy all your cravings."
—Juli Huss, author of *The Faux Gourmet*

TODD WILBUR is the author of *Top Secret Recipes, More Top Secret
Recipes, Top Secret Restaurant Recipes,* and *Top Secret Recipes Lite!* (all
available from Plume). When not taste-testing recipes on himself, his
friends, or TV talk-show hosts, Todd lives in Las Vegas.

ALSO BY TODD WILBUR

Top Secret Recipes
More Top Secret Recipes
Top Secret Restaurant Recipes
Top Secret Recipes Lite!

To radio's Buzz Burbank.
And his colon.

THANK YOU . . .

To everyone at Penguin / Putnam for all of your support through the years on each of the *Top Secret Recipes* books.

To Marilyn Hart and Kate Baltz for their incredible help and fresh ideas in the kitchen.

To my loving family and dear friends for all the kind words in times of need.

To Zebu, the Wonder Dog, for always being there. And rarely moving.

To the love of my life, Pamela. I couldn't have gotten through it without you. Every day with you is an adventure, every night is a dream come true.

CONTENTS

LOW-FAT TOP SECRET RECIPES CONVERSIONS

A Word From
Fat Gram Freddy

To all you beautiful people, I extend a greasy "hello," and my most heartfelt plea. My name is Fat Gram Freddy, and I am exactly one gram of pure, glistening fat. I slide onto these pages before you as the spokesfat for trillions and trillions of others just like me who can no longer congeal idly by as our kind succumb in great numbers to all the senseless digestion. For many years it appeared you were on the right track. But I'm afraid that a recent about-face is returning us to the days when a fat gram's existence is in a constant and tragic state of jeopardy.

Todd has been kind enough to allow me an open forum here in his new low-fat *Top Secret Recipes* cookbook to urge for a return to discretion in the consumption of my fatty brethren. He has allowed me to speak freely and has promised not to edit these thoughts—the first recorded words ever to be penned by a modestly handsome gram of fat—as long as I attempt to stay concise, reasonably polite, and off his new couch.

I assure you that I'm literate. I'm sincere. And, yes, I do wonders for fettucine alfredo and chicken wings. I'm told I make a lot of sense when I focus, so please read carefully these words I write.

Look, I know you like me ... you really like me. None of us can deny that fact. But just because I feel so good slipping over your tongue and down into the dark depths of your throat doesn't mean that my friends and I should be ingested in such massive amounts with every single snack and meal. Why not have an apple the next time that acid-filled torture chamber you people call a stomach begins its terrifying growl? I hear that the broccoli and tomatoes are fantastic this year. Heck, we've always stayed away from those wonderful foods unless you invite us. That's just how we are.

We fat grams have shared a lot of joy in the past decade as most of you worked hard to consume products created with little or none of us. We rejoiced in the early '90s as this trend encouraged manufacturers to go nuts creating entire product lines of scrumptious low-fat meals and fat-free snacks. It was beautiful! This helped many of us to survive, uneaten, for long periods of time.

But the dark clouds formed once again as the millennium came to a close. Toward the end of the '90s, low-fat food sales began to slump, and now my slippery amigos are once again disappearing at an alarming rate.

This tragic turn has left us all in a state of panic. I'm afraid that one day, very soon now, it'll be time for yours truly to take the one-way drive down Digestive Tract Highway. That is why I am now appealing to you for help ... by merely helping yourselves.

HOW IT ALL WENT DOWN

I remember like it was yesterday. Right after your second big war, I watched in terror as buddies of mine got slathered on toast, glopped over salads, smeared over pizza, and dolloped onto desserts in numbers that would make your fork spin.

Turns out you indulged in rich, creamy foods without any regard for content or consequence. Your average consumption of fat at this ghastly time reached 40 percent of calories. That's one of the highest percentages in history. It looked like you folks were on some kind of wild, self-destructive tear.

What you didn't realize was that all the fat grams you were sucking down couldn't just sit back and take the absorption without exacting a devious revenge with their dying breath. As you snarfed on my fellow fat boys, they went to work from the inside, raising your cholesterol, attacking your arteries, and making you all flabby and swollen. The deadly chain reaction that followed was devastating to your life support system. We were at war, and our troops were required to use cruel, desperate measures. With each choked artery and every seized heart we claimed another victory.

This battle raged on in your inner space for many years, until you were finally tipped off to our clandestine scheme.

In the '60s, the intelligence officers you call "doctors" detected our internal attack and sent out the alarm. You had no choice but to cut back on the massive consumption of my compadres by propagating a campaign to reduce the intake of fat in the American diet. Lower-fat dairy products were introduced and lean meat hit your grocery stores. For us, it was a glorious time; yet only a momentary victory.

Through the next several decades you worked hard to create edibles of all kinds, containing fewer of my kind. This trend escalated in the '90s as companies with names such as Nabisco, ConAgra, Quaker Oats, Keebler, Weight Watchers, Hostess, and Hershey had the heart to give you munchies that didn't rely on fat grams to appeal to that slimy, bud-covered muscle in your cavernous pie holes.

We thought that this change in your eating habits signaled the end of our fight for survival. What we failed to notice over the years, however, was the sedentary lifestyle you humans had been creating for yourselves. Homes were made to be more comfortable. Cars clogged up the roadways. Television, movies, and video games were developing into multibillion-dollar industries that required—even encouraged—an increasing amount of inactivity. Fat or no fat, this was the recipe for your doom. Yet you were still placing the blame on us.

Recently I took it upon my oily self to do a little research, and I found that in 1986 the census bureau determined that 52 percent of Americans were fat. This bloated condition—which you curiously named after us—would continue to spread through the years, even though record numbers of low-fat and fat-free products had been distributed amongst you.

As 1998 rolled around, the percentage was up. The bulges

affected an astounding 68 percent of you, with 22 percent referred to as "obese." Using a simple spreadsheet, I ran these figures through my laptop and came up with a shocking projection: If this rate continues, 100 percent of you will be obese by the year 2230!

So what's happening? Is it that you thought the low-fat and fat-free labels on all those products gave you the freedom to gorge? Your U.S. Department of Agriculture checked out the average American diet and found that even with the abundance of lower-fat products on store shelves the total amount of fat in most diets in the late 90s was the same as in the 60s, and in some cases even went up. And according to the USDA, total caloric intake was increasing, mostly from sugar and carbohydrates. Oh, and booze. Apparently eating lots of lower-fat food makes you want to get a buzz on.

I checked out Michael Fumento's book, *The Fat of the Land,* and he says the new lower-fat foods are so boring that many of you figure, like whales inhaling krill, that if you eat enough of it, somewhere in there might be a tasty morsel. You were often disappointed with what you fished out.

When you switched to lower-fat products and experienced no weight loss, you figured the food was to blame. You may have given no regard to the increased amount of low-fat foods you consumed or to the decrease in your weight-shedding activity. You decided that eating foods less appealing to the palate was pointless, so you happily returned back to mowing down the fat grams. Except now the food was chased with a good dose of guilt and regret.

Friends, this is no way for you to live. That is why Fat Gram Freddy has come to the rescue.

THE SOLUTION—
FROM A FAT GRAM WHO CARES

Yes indeed, 1998 was a dark year for fat grams everywhere. This was the year that food manufacturers attempted to revive sluggish sales of lower-fat products by putting more of us fat grams back in. Manufacturers realized that since you folks didn't see any weight-loss effects from eating the fat-free stuff, you started reevaluating your purchases. You figured if the weight loss never kicked in, you might as well return to a more stimulating eating experience.

The flavorlessness of many fat-free and low-fat products turned off consumers who decided that they would rather purchase products with moderate fat reduction or no fat reduction at all. Sure, I'll admit that some of that low-fat stuff tastes worse than the box it's packed in, but there are plenty of others out there that taste great. And improved products are still unveiled as manufacturers learn new, tasty, fat-saving tricks in the test kitchens.

But is it too late? My biggest fear is that most of you are tired of wasting money trying to figure out which lower-fat foods taste good and which don't. You aren't interested in playing the supermarket crapshoot, even when the food is not at the core of the problem.

The real problem, according to this other book I read called *The Skinny on Fat,* is that we have become a sedentary society. One-quarter of Americans are slugs. Too many of you make a habit of planting yourself in front of the television with salty snacks and plates of food, getting up only to replenish the rations or expel them.

In *The Skinny on Fat,* Shawna Vogel says, "Watching TV slows down a person's metabolism to the point where they expend less energy than if they were doing nothing at all. Television, through its advertisements, can also increase the amount people eat while they're watching. And if eating in front of the TV is common, then it can become a conditioned stimulus to eat."

According to *U.S. News & World Report,* only 15 percent of you get enough heart-strengthening aerobic exercise to live a long, healthy life. With work and family pressures and such easy access to engaging yet passive entertainment, you rarely make exercise a number-one priority.

Everyone in the know seems to be in agreement. When you exercise, or at least make an effort to participate in some sort of activity that hoists you off the posterior, you feel better about yourself and tend to eat better. Next time, perhaps you'll park your car a few blocks from your destination and walk, or maybe you can take the stairs once in while rather than the elevator. When you feel better about yourself, you'll be more likely to leave us fat grams alone.

And remember this: Diets rarely work. Don't even put that pressure on yourself. It's been shown over and over again that when dieters deny themselves the food they love to eat, it has a negative emotional impact. Sure, a few pounds may be shed early on, but there's usually a relapse on the horizon that will bring back those lost pounds and then some. A University of Toronto psychologist discovered that people rarely get fat from going on binges, but rather binge because they have been depriving themselves on a restrictive diet.

That cool Shawna Vogel book I mentioned earlier cites the fact that diet programs like Jenny Craig and Nutri/System have seen revenues plunge in recent years because "too much emphasis has been placed on restriction dieting and weight loss as the keys to health and not enough on activity, weight maintenance and metabolic fitness."

I realize I'm no picture of health—I'm made of pure fat for God's sake, so I think I have a pretty good excuse—but food and dieting is my business; it's all I know. And all I'm hearing lately is that you've got to get into a little activity each and every day. Or at least thirty minutes of exercise three or four times a week. Get over the obsession with dieting and thinness and have a burger once in a while if you like. It's not going to kill you. Then for other meals you can get back to fat-free and low-fat products, and eat those in moderation, too. Eat the kind of stuff made from this book, so that you will enjoy the experience. That's why Todd put it here.

WHY THIS BOOK ROCKS

From what Todd has shown me, this book proves that reduced-fat food doesn't have to taste like cardboard. The recipes here create the type of food you would love to eat with less fat and more taste. It's the kind of stuff that satisfies your taste buds by replacing fat with other carefully crafted ingredients. My buddies and I like that.

With this book you'll discover tricks for mixing up fat-free dressings using pectin and cornstarch. And a way to bake chicken so that it has a deep-fried texture and no skin. You'll also discover Todd's unique technique for using the microwave to make a fat-free cookie filling that looks and tastes just like the stuff inside an Oreo.

You'll notice that Todd's divided the book into two sections: "Clones," for re-creating kitchen copies of your favorite foods that are already low in fat grams, such as Nabisco Honey Maid Grahams, Gardenburgers, and SnackWell's products. And "Conversions," for creating reduced-fat clones of your normally fat-filled favorites, such as Chili's Southwestern Eggrolls, Wendy's Spicy Chicken Sandwich, and McDonald's Egg McMuffin. These conversions will let you enjoy the taste of your favorite products for which reduced-fat versions don't exist in stores. And just about all of these recipes cut fat from the real thing by at least half, sometimes by much more than that. To help you keep track, you'll find fat and calories counted at the bottom of each recipe.

I know that you can never entirely give up eating us fat grams. I understand that you need me and my kind in your diet to survive. Your huge bodies require the vitamins and fatty acids that we provide. But just because a package of cookies says "reduced fat" on the label doesn't mean you can eat a half a bag a day. There are still a lot of us little fellers in a quadruple-serving nosh fest. Not to mention a ton of those other guys, the calories.

Don't lose confidence that low-fat food can help you maintain a great physique when enjoyed in reasonable amounts. But remember that weight loss or maintenance cannot be realized in diet alone.

I speak for fat grams everywhere when I say that we will very much appreciate your efforts to return to eating lower-fat foods. When you're at the grocery store, please grab for the packages with the green "low-fat" labels again, and give those products another chance.

Better yet, when you have a craving for the oral sensation of a food that bursts with fat grams, open the pages of this fine book and satisfy your palate with some reduced-fat clones. The food will quell your craving, and your efforts will be rewarded. The process of cooking this food and shopping for the ingredients will keep you off the sofa. And that's a good thing.

Ladies and gentlemen, this is my message. It's a simple one. Eat more of the stuff on these pages … and eat less of me. It's for your own good, and mine.

I'm a fat gram. I know what I'm talking about.

Thank you.

—Fat Gram Freddy

P.S. Todd wants me to remind you that you can find tons of additional secret clone recipes on his free Web site at:

http://www.topsecretrecipes.com

You can even contact him with suggestions for other recipes to clone at:

Todd@topsecretrecipes.com

Tell him Fat Gram Freddy sent you.

LOW-FAT
TOP
SECRET
RECIPES
CLONES

TOP SECRET RECIPES
VERSION OF

APPLEBEE'S LOW-FAT ASIAN CHICKEN SALAD

☆ ✄ ✵ ✎ ◉ ✂ ☞

My new diet plan is called the Chopsticks Diet. It requires that you use only chopsticks to eat everything: spaghetti, peas, hamburgers, cookies, ice cream, salads—whatever. As the food slips off the chopsticks, the pounds slip off of you. It's especially effective if you've never used chopsticks before. For those who can use them well, you've got to switch to the other hand. If you're Asian, you're only allowed to use one.

As the seasons change, so does the menu at this popular, casual, restaurant chain. You'll find this item in the "Low-Fat and Fabulous" column of the menu during the summer months where it's been a favorite since 1997. As with any salad, the waistline violator is the traditionally fat-filled dressing that is drizzled in gobs over the top of very healthy greens (a tablespoon of dressing usually contains around ten to twelve grams of fat). So if we can just figure out a cool way to make the dressing fat-free, we're well on our way to making a huge salad—four of them to be exact—with only twelve grams of fat on each plate. Most of those grams come from the chicken breast, and the crunchy chow mein noodles pick up the rest.

Just be sure to plan ahead when you make this one. The chicken should marinate for a few hours if you want it to taste like the original. Hope you're hungry.

I cup teriyaki marinade   4 skinless chicken breast fillets

FAT-FREE ASIAN DRESSING

2 cups water	1 teaspoon salt
½ cup granulated sugar	¼ teaspoon garlic powder
3 tablespoons dry pectin	¼ teaspoon ground black
1 tablespoon white vinegar	pepper
½ teaspoon soy sauce	¼ teaspoon paprika

8 cups chopped romaine lettuce	2 cups shredded carrots
8 cups chopped iceberg lettuce	1 cup chopped green onion
3 cups shredded red cabbage	1⅓ cups crispy chow mein
3 cups shredded green cabbage	noodles

1. Combine teriyaki marinade and chicken breasts in a medium bowl or resealable plastic bag. Marinate chicken for 3 to 4 hours.

2. Prepare the dressing by combining all of the ingredients in a small saucepan over medium heat. Bring mixture to a rolling boil while stirring often with a whisk, then remove the pan from the heat to cool. When the dressing has cooled, pour it into a covered container and chill.

3. When chicken breasts have marinated, preheat barbecue grill to high heat. Grill chicken for 3 to 4 minutes per side or until done.

4. Combine the romaine and iceberg lettuce, red and green cabbage, and 1 cup of shredded carrots in a large bowl with the dressing. Toss well.

5. Divide the tossed greens among four plates. Sprinkle ¼ cup of green onions over each salad, followed by ⅓ cup of crispy chow mein noodles.

6. When the chicken breasts are done, slice each one, widthwise, into bite-size pieces. Sprinkle the sliced chicken breasts over each salad.

7. Place a ¼-cup pile of shredded carrots in the center of each salad.

• SERVES 4 AS AN ENTRÉE.

Nutrition Facts

SERVING SIZE—1 SALAD	FAT (PER SERVING)—12 G
TOTAL SERVINGS—4	CALORIES (PER SERVING)—575

• • • •

TOP SECRET RECIPES
VERSION OF

APPLEBEE'S LOW-FAT & FABULOUS BROWNIE SUNDAE

☆   🖑   💣   🗡   ◉   ✂   ☞

The Applebee's chain is now the world's largest casual dining restaurant, with over one thousand units in seven countries and forty-eight states. In less than four years, the chain has doubled in size. That's great if you're a restaurant chain, but put enough fat-filled desserts in your belly, and you'll double in size, too.

That's why we're happy to see items like this one on the menu. It tastes like a decadent, guilty pleasure, but it actually contains only four grams of fat per serving. This is possible because the brownie "pie" is made in a special way using a combination of low-fat and fat-free chocolates, some egg whites, and just a bit of shortening. Grab yourself some fat-free frozen yogurt, and share this one with eight hungry friends.

LOW-FAT BROWNIE

2 egg whites	1 teaspoon vanilla
¾ cup granulated sugar	1 ½ cups all-purpose flour
2 tablespoons shortening	¼ cup cocoa
½ cup Hershey's chocolate syrup	¾ teaspoon salt
½ cup fudge topping	¼ teaspoon baking soda
¼ cup warm water	2 teaspoons chopped walnuts
9 scoops fat-free vanilla frozen yogurt	chocolate syrup, heated

1. Preheat oven to 350 degrees.
2. Make the brownie cake by whipping the egg whites in a large bowl (not plastic) with an electric mixer until they become thick.
3. Add the sugar to the egg whites and continue beating until the mixture forms soft peaks.
4. To the egg white and sugar mixture, add the shortening, chocolate syrup, fudge, water, and vanilla.
5. In a separate bowl, combine the flour, cocoa, salt, and baking soda.
6. While beating the wet mixture, slowly add the dry mixture and mix until smooth.
7. Lightly grease a 9-inch pie pan with shortening. Pour the brownie batter into the pan and sprinkle the chopped walnuts over the top. Bake for 35 minutes or until a toothpick poked into the center comes out clean.
8. When the brownie pie has cooled a bit, slice it into 9 equal pie-shaped portions.
9. Arrange a slice of the low-fat brownie pie on a plate next to a scoop of vanilla frozen yogurt.
10. Drizzle the warmed chocolate sauce over the top of the brownie and frozen yogurt, and serve.

- MAKES 9 DESSERTS.

Nutrition Facts

| SERVING SIZE—1 DESSERT | FAT (PER SERVING)—4 G |
| TOTAL SERVINGS—9 | CALORIES (PER SERVING)—424 |

• • • •

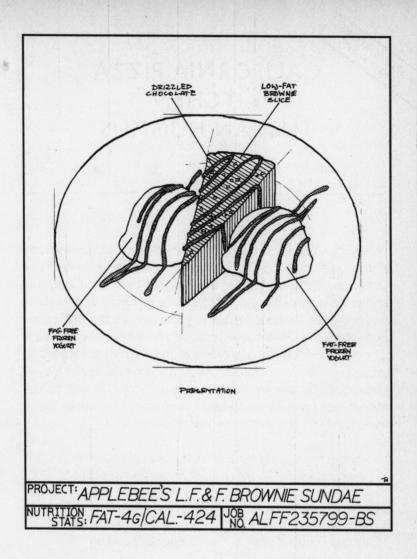

DRIZZLED
CHOCOLATE

LOW-FAT
BROWNIE
SLICE

FAT-FREE
FROZEN
YOGURT

FAT-FREE
FROZEN
YOGURT

PRESENTATION

PROJECT: *APPLEBEE'S L.F.& F. BROWNIE SUNDAE*

NUTRITION
STATS: *FAT-4g/CAL.-424* JOB
NO. *ALFF235799-BS*

TOP SECRET RECIPES
VERSION OF

CALIFORNIA PIZZA KITCHEN TUSCAN HUMMUS

Nowhere could I find the "Tuscan white bean," or any mention of it in research materials. But there it is in the California Pizza Kitchen menu description for this delicious hummus. Could this just be the chain's fancy way of describing garbanzo beans, otherwise known as chickpeas? After all, garbanzos are the only beans used for any traditional hummus recipe, and they seemed to work perfectly in this low-fat re-creation of the chain's tasty appetizer. Just be sure you have a good food processor to puree all the ingredients. If you have trouble finding sesame tahini in your supermarket, check out your local health food store. And while you're there, see if you can spot those Tuscan white beans.

1 15-ounce can garbanzo beans
   (strain and keep ¼ cup of
   liquid)
¼ cup liquid from the can
¼ cup fresh lemon juice
3 tablespoons sesame tahini
2 teaspoons minced garlic

1 teaspoon granulated sugar
¾ teaspoon white pepper
½ teaspoon salt
¼ teaspoon cumin
⅛ teaspoon cayenne pepper
⅛ teaspoon paprika

OPTIONAL GARNISH
2 tablespoons chopped Roma
   tomatoes

pinch fresh basil
pinch chopped fresh garlic

warm pita bread slices

1. Dump the entire contents of the can of garbanzo beans into a strainer set over a bowl. Let the beans sit for a little while so that all of the liquid drips into the bowl.
2. Dump the beans and ¼ cup of the liquid from the bowl into a food processor.
3. Add the remaining ingredients to the food processor, and puree the mixture until completely smooth—about a minute or so.
4. Spoon the hummus into a covered container and chill for at least 2 hours so that the flavors can develop. When serving, you may wish to garnish the hummus with a couple table-spoons of chopped Roma tomatoes mixed with a dash of chopped fresh basil and garlic. Serve with warm, sliced pita bread or your choice of chips or crackers.

• MAKES 1¾ CUPS.

Nutrition Facts

SERVING SIZE—2 TABLESPOONS	FAT (PER SERVING)—2.5 G
TOTAL SERVINGS—14	CALORIES (PER SERVING)—48

• • • •

CALIFORNIA PIZZA KITCHEN DAKOTA SMASHED PEA & BARLEY SOUP

☆   ✄   ✿   ✎   ☯   ✂   ☞

Got one of those cool hand blenders? You know, the kind of gadget that used to be pitched on those annoying yet compelling late-night infomercials? It comes in handy for this recipe, which requires the split peas to be smashed into a smooth consistency, just like the original. If you don't have a hand mixer, a standard blender works just fine. This soup is very tasty and very low in fat. And the barley gives it a special chunky consistency and added flavor that aren't found in most pea soups. If you want to go even lower in fat, use fat-free chicken broth instead of the regular stuff, then run in place with a can in each hand to burn some extra calories.

2 cups split peas
6 cups water
2 14½-ounce cans chicken broth
    (4 cups)
⅓ cup minced onion
1 large clove garlic, minced
2 teaspoons lemon juice
1 teaspoon salt
1 teaspoon granulated sugar

¼ teaspoon dried parsley
⅛ teaspoon white pepper
dash dried thyme
½ cup barley
6 cups water
2 medium carrots, diced (about
    1 cup)
½ stalk celery (¼ cup)

GARNISH
chopped green onion

1. Rinse and drain the split peas, then add them to a large pot with 6 cups of water, chicken broth, onion, garlic, lemon juice, salt, sugar, parsley, pepper, and thyme. Bring to a boil, then reduce heat and simmer for 75 to 90 minutes or until the peas are soft and the soup is thick.
2. While the peas are cooking, combine the barley with 6 cups of water, carrots, and celery in a saucepan. Bring to a boil, then reduce heat and also simmer for 75 to 90 minutes or until the barley is soft and most of the water has been absorbed.
3. When the split pea mixture has become a thick soup, use a handheld blender to puree the peas until the mixture is smooth. You may also use a standard blender or food processor for this step, pureeing the soup in batches. Alternately, if you like, you may skip this step, keeping the soup rather chunky. It's still good, just not as smooth as the real thing.
4. Drain the barley mixture in a sieve or colander and add it to the split pea mixture. Continue to simmer for about 15 minutes, stirring occasionally. Turn off the heat, cover the soup, and let it sit for 15 minutes before serving.

- MAKES 8 CUPS.

Nutrition Facts

SERVING SIZE—2 CUPS	FAT (PER SERVING)—3 G
TOTAL SERVINGS—4	CALORIES (PER SERVING)—450

• • • •

TOP SECRET RECIPES VERSION OF

CALIFORNIA PIZZA KITCHEN GRILLED EGGPLANT CHEESELESS PIZZA

☆   ✌   💣   ✎   ☯   ✂   ☞

When PepsiCo shelled out $100 million for a 67 percent share of the trendy pizza chain back in 1992, founders Lawrence Flax and Richard Rosenfield thought they had it made. Unfortunately, the company behind Pizza Hut found expanding the more up-scale eatery an unfamiliar struggle. The company expanded too quickly (Planet Hollywood, anyone?), and as costs began to dwarf sales figures, fresh ingredients were replaced with cheaper frozen products. Customers noticed, and sales took a nosedive. By 1996, PepsiCo decided to bail.

The following year, PepsiCo's share of the chain was picked up by New York investment firm Rosser, Sherrill & Co. Fresh ingredients returned to the kitchens, and the size of the pizzas was increased without adjusting the price. Sales once again blossomed, and the chain was on its way back to turning its first profit since 1991.

Here's a great pizza to clone if you need to take a little time off from delicious-yet-fat-filled mozzarella cheese. With the marinated, grilled eggplant and tasty honey-wheat dough, you won't even miss that gooey white stuff. Be sure to start this one a day before you plan to eat it. The dough needs that long to rise in the fridge for just the right California Pizza Kitchen–like consistency.

HONEY-WHEAT DOUGH

⅓ cup plus 1 tablespoon warm
    water (105 to 115 degrees F)
1 tablespoon honey
¾ teaspoon yeast

⅔ cup bread flour
⅓ cup whole wheat flour
½ teaspoon salt
½ tablespoon olive oil

TOPPING

1½ tablespoons soy sauce
1 tablespoon olive oil
⅛ teaspoon cayenne pepper
⅛ teaspoon garlic powder
⅛ teaspoon cumin
½ eggplant, sliced lengthwise ¼
    inch thick

¼ medium red onion, sliced into
    thin rings (about ½ cup)
1 teaspoon minced fresh cilantro
1½ to 2 cups fresh spinach,
    chopped into thin strips
⅓ cup reconstituted sun-dried
    tomatoes,* sliced into strips

OPTIONAL

fat-free vinaigrette

1. Prepare the pizza dough by combining the water with the honey and yeast in a small bowl or measuring cup. Stir until the yeast is dissolved, then let the mixture sit for 5 minutes until the surface turns foamy. (If it doesn't foam, either the yeast was too old or the water was too hot. Try again.) Sift the flours and salt together in a medium bowl. Make a depression in the flour and pour the olive oil and yeast mixture into it. Use a fork or spoon to stir the liquid, gradually drawing in more flour as you stir, until all the ingredients are combined. At this point you will have to use your hands to blend the dough until it is smooth and to form it into a ball. Knead the dough with the heels of your hands on a lightly floured surface for 10 minutes or until the texture of the dough is smooth and elastic. Form the dough back into a ball, coat it lightly with oil, and place it into a clean bowl covered with plastic wrap. Keep the dough in a warm place for about 2 hours to allow the dough to double in size. Punch the dough

*Heat a couple cups of water to boiling in the microwave. Add 6 to 8 sun-dried tomato slices to the water and let them sit for about ½ hour. Remove the slices and drain on paper towels until you need them.

down and put it back into the covered bowl and back into the refrigerator overnight. Take the dough from the refrigerator 1 to 2 hours before you plan to build the pizza so that the dough can warm up to room temperature.

2. When you're ready to make your pizza, preheat the oven to 500 degrees. If you have a pizza stone, now's the time to use it.

3. Preheat barbecue grill to high temperature.

4. Combine the soy sauce with 1 tablespoon of olive oil, cayenne pepper, garlic powder, and cumin in a small bowl.

5. Brush the entire surface of each eggplant slice with this soy sauce mixture. Make sure you have some left over.

6. Grill the eggplant slices for 2 to 3 minutes per side, then remove them from the grill to cool.

7. On a lightly floured surface, form the pizza dough into a circle with an approximately 10-inch diameter. Be sure to form a lip around the edge.

8. Brush the top surface of the pizza dough with the remaining soy sauce mixture.

9. Arrange the red onion slices over the pizza dough.

10. The eggplant slices go on the pizza next, then toss the pizza into the oven on a pizza pan, or directly onto a pizza stone. Bake for 10 to 12 minutes or until the crust is light brown and crispy. Pop any bubbles in the crust that may form as the pizza bakes.

11. Remove the pizza from the oven and sprinkle cilantro over the top.

12. Slice the pizza into 6 even slices with a sharp pizza wheel.

13. Sprinkle the thinly chopped spinach over the top of the pizza.

14. Sprinkle the sun-dried tomato strips over the top.

15. Serve pizza with the optional vinaigrette on the side.

• MAKES 1 10-INCH PIZZA.

Nutrition Facts

SERVING SIZE—3 SLICES   FAT (PER SERVING)—8 G
TOTAL SERVINGS—2   CALORIES (PER SERVING)—380

• • • •

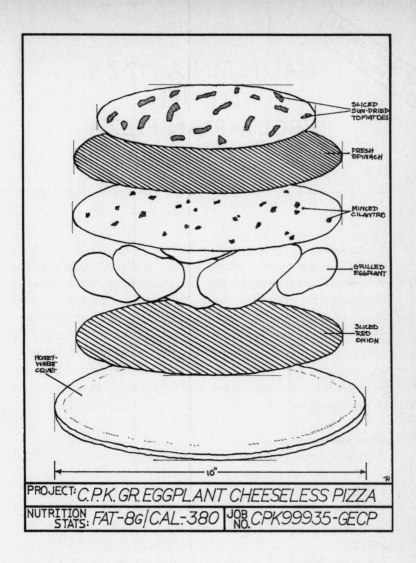

SLICED
SUN-DRIED
TOMATOES

FRESH
SPINACH

MINCED
CILANTRO

GRILLED
EGGPLANT

SLICED
RED
ONION

HONEY-
WHEAT
CRUST

10"

PROJECT: C.P.K. GR. EGGPLANT CHEESELESS PIZZA

NUTRITION STATS: FAT-8g/CAL.-380   JOB NO. CPK99935-GECP

CALIFORNIA PIZZA KITCHEN VEGETARIAN PIZZA

☆　　✂　　☙　　✐　　◉　　✂　　☞

Who needs to cook with animal parts when you can make a pizza taste like this? It's grilled veggies and mozzarella cheese stacked on a great clone for the chain's tasty honey-wheat dough. With regular mozzarella cheese, the total fat for three slices comes in at around nineteen grams, which is still much less than you'd get from, say, the pepperoni-topped variety (tipping the scales at about fifteen grams *per slice*). Just remember to prepare your dough a day before you plan to make the pizza. This way you'll get the best consistency in the final product. And one heck of a better clone.

HONEY-WHEAT DOUGH

⅓ cup plus I tablespoon warm
　　water (105 to 115 degrees F)
I tablespoon honey
¾ teaspoon yeast

⅔ cup bread flour
⅓ cup whole wheat flour
½ teaspoon salt
½ tablespoon olive oil

SAUCE

I teaspoon olive oil
I tablespoon minced white
　　onion
I clove garlic, minced
I tomato, chopped
I 15-ounce can tomato sauce

2 teaspoons granulated sugar
¼ teaspoon dried oregano
¼ teaspoon dried basil
¼ teaspoon salt
⅛ teaspoon dried thyme
dash ground black pepper

1 ½ tablespoons soy sauce
1 tablespoon olive oil
⅛ teaspoon cayenne pepper
⅛ teaspoon garlic powder .
⅛ teaspoon cumin
½ eggplant, sliced lengthwise
    ¼ inch thick
1 cup shredded mozzarella
    cheese

¾ cup mushrooms, sliced thin
    (2 to 3 mushrooms)
⅓ medium onion, sliced into thin
    rings (about ⅔ cup)
⅓ cup reconstituted sun-dried
    tomatoes,* sliced into strips
1 ½ cups steamed broccoli florets
    (bite-size)
1 teaspoon minced fresh oregano

1. Prepare the pizza dough by following step #1 from page 21.
2. When you are ready to make the pizza, preheat oven to 500 degrees. Use a pizza stone if you have one.
3. Prepare the sauce by first heating the olive oil over medium heat in a medium saucepan. Sauté the onion and garlic for 1 minute in the oil. Add the tomato and sauté for an additional minute before adding the remaining sauce ingredients to the pan. Bring the sauce to a boil, then reduce heat and simmer for 20 to 30 minutes, or until thicker. Cover the sauce until it is needed.
4. Preheat barbecue grill to high temperature.
5. Combine the soy sauce with 1 tablespoon olive oil, cayenne pepper, garlic powder, and cumin in a small bowl.
6. Brush the entire surface of the eggplant with the soy sauce mixture. Grill the eggplant slices for 2 to 3 minutes per side, then remove the slices from the heat and set them aside until they are needed.
7. On a lightly floured surface, form the pizza dough into a circle that is approximately 10 inches across.
8. Spread about ½ cup of the sauce evenly over the surface of the dough.
9. Arrange the grilled eggplant on the pizza, then sprinkle the cheese evenly over the top of the eggplant.

*Heat a couple cups of water to boiling in the microwave. Add 6 to 8 sun-dried tomato slices to the water and let them sit for about ½ hour. Remove and drain the slices on paper towels until you need them.

10. Next sprinkle the mushrooms onto the pizza, followed by the onion slices.
11. Sprinkle the sun-dried tomato slices on the pizza, followed by the broccoli florets.
12. Bake the pizza for 10 to 12 minutes or until the crust is light brown and the cheese begins to bubble. Pop any bubbles in the crust that may form as the pizza bakes.
13. Remove the pizza from the oven and sprinkle the fresh oregano over the top. Use a pizza wheel to slice the pizza into 6 pieces and serve.

• MAKES 1 10-INCH PIZZA.

Nutrition Facts

SERVING SIZE—3 SLICES　　　　FAT (PER SERVING)—19 G
TOTAL SERVINGS—2　　　　　　CALORIES (PER SERVING)—632

•　•　•　•

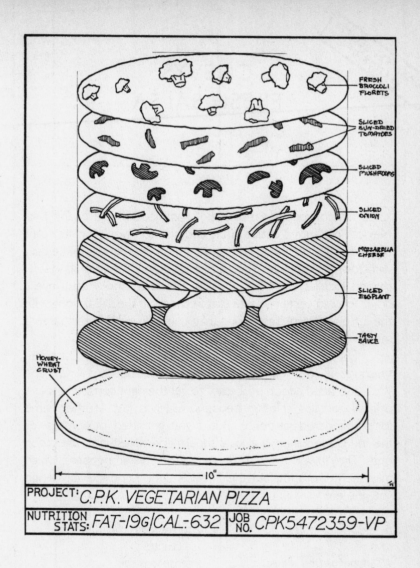

FRESH
BROCCOLI
FLORETS

SLICED
SUN-DRIED
TOMATOES

SLICED
MUSHROOMS

SLICED
ONION

MOZZARELLA
CHEESE

SLICED
EGGPLANT

TASTY
SAUCE

HONEY-
WHEAT
CRUST

|← 10" →|

PROJECT: *C.P.K. VEGETARIAN PIZZA*

NUTRITION STATS: *FAT-19G/CAL.-632*   **JOB NO.** *CPK5472359-VP*

CHEVYS
FRESH SALSA

☆   ✌   ✺   ✎   ☯   ✂   ☞

Chevys's concept of Fresh Mex® has made it one of the best Mexican restaurant chains in the country. You won't find any cans of food in the kitchen since every item on the menu is made daily with fresh ingredients. The restaurant claims it makes its heart-shaped tortillas each day, and this delicious, smoky salsa every hour. You can certainly taste that freshness in the salsa, along with the unique mesquite flavors that come from the restaurant's mesquite-fire grill.

For this clone you won't need a mesquite grill, just some mesquite liquid smoke flavoring and a hot barbecue grill. Oh, and you'll also need a food processor to get the right consistency. The original contains chipotle peppers, which is just another name for smoked red jalapeños. But if you get tired of hunting for the red jalapeños in your local supermarkets, just grab the green ones. They'll work fine. You'll need a total of ten peppers, which may seem like a lot, but their heat is tamed considerably when you grill 'em.

6 medium tomatoes
olive oil
10 jalapeños (red is best)
¼ medium Spanish
    onion
2 cloves garlic

2 tablespoons chopped fresh
    cilantro
2 teaspoons salt
2 tablespoons white vinegar
1½ teaspoons mesquite-flavored
    liquid smoke

1. Preheat your barbecue grill to high temperature.
2. Remove any stems from the tomatoes, then rub some oil

over each tomato. You can leave the stems on the jalapeños for now.

3. Place the tomatoes on the grill when it's hot. After about 10 minutes, place all of the jalapeños onto the grill. In about 10 minutes you can turn the tomatoes and the peppers. When nearly the entire surface of the peppers has charred black, you can remove them from the grill. The tomatoes will turn black partially, but when the skin begins to come off they're done. Put the peppers and tomatoes on a plate and let them cool.

4. When the tomatoes and peppers have cooled, remove most of the skin from the tomatoes and place them into a food processor. Pinch the stem off the end of the peppers and place them into the food processor as well. Don't include the liquid left on the plate. Toss that out.

5. Add the remaining ingredients to the food processor and puree on high speed for 5 to 10 seconds or until the mixture has a smooth consistency.

6. Place the salsa into a covered container and chill for several hours or overnight while the flavors develop.

- MAKES 2 CUPS.

Nutrition Facts

SERVING SIZE—2 TABLESPOONS	FAT (PER SERVING)—0 G
TOTAL SERVINGS—16	CALORIES (PER SERVING)—10

• • • •

TOP SECRET RECIPES VERSION OF

ENTENMANN'S LIGHT LOW-FAT CINNAMON RAISIN SWEET ROLLS

☆　✂　💣　✒　☯　✂　☞

Entenmann's was one of the first on the block to throw irresistible, low-fat versions of its delicious baked goods in front of us at the supermarket. The company's specialty is its low-fat sweet cinnamon rolls that taste as good as any of the full-fat varieties produced by other established brands. These rolls are so good that I'm presenting clones for two varieties. This recipe is for the smaller of the two and includes raisins for those of you who like shriveled grapes in your pastry. If you want bigger cinnamon rolls sans the mini prunes, check out the next recipe.

ROLLS

2 teaspoons yeast
½ cup warm water
¼ cup granulated sugar
1⅔ cups bread flour

½ teaspoon baking powder
¼ teaspoon salt
2 tablespoons shortening, melted
3 tablespoons egg substitute

FILLING

¼ cup fat-free butter-flavored
    spread
⅓ cup light brown sugar

2 tablespoons Wondra flour
2 teaspoons cinnamon
¼ cup raisins

ICING

½ cup powdered sugar
2 tablespoons fat-free cream
    cheese

couple drops vanilla extract
dash salt

1. Dissolve the yeast in the warm water. When the yeast is dissolved, add the sugar and stir until it is dissolved as well. In about 5 minutes, foam will form on the surface. (If foam does not form, your yeast may be too old or the water may be too hot. Try again.)
2. In a large bowl, mix together the flour, baking powder, and salt.
3. Melt the shortening in the microwave, set on high, for about 1 minute. Add the melted shortening, egg substitute, and yeast mixture to the flour, and stir by hand until all ingredients are combined. Use your hands to knead the dough for about 5 minutes, then form it into a ball and put it into a covered bowl in a warm spot for 1 to 1½ hours or until it doubles in size.
4. Roll dough out onto a floured surface so that it is a rectangle measuring 12 inches wide and 18 inches long.
5. Use a spatula to spread the butter-flavored spread evenly over the surface of the dough. Combine the brown sugar, Wondra flour, and cinnamon in a small bowl. Spread this mixture evenly over the surface of the dough. Sprinkle the raisins evenly over the filling.
6. Starting from the top edge, roll the dough down until it forms a long roll. Cut off the ends, then slice the dough into 12 even slices and arrange them, cut side down, in an 9 x 13-inch greased baking pan or dish. Cover the pan with plastic wrap and let the rolls rise again for another 1 to 1½ hours in a warm place.
7. Preheat oven to 400 degrees.
8. Remove the plastic from the pan and bake the rolls for 18 to 22 minutes or until brown.
9. As rolls bake, combine the icing ingredients in a medium bowl with an electric mixer. Mix on high speed for about 1 minute.
10. When rolls are cool, spread icing over the top of each one. Cover the baking dish, and store the rolls at room temperature until you are ready to serve them.

- MAKES 12 ROLLS.

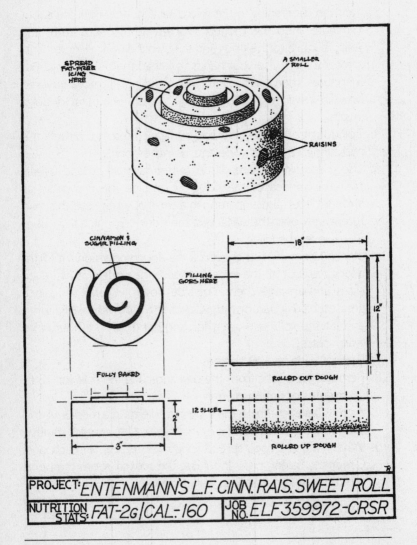

SPREAD FAT-FREE ICING HERE

A SMALLER ROLL

RAISINS

CINNAMON & SUGAR FILLING

FILLING GOES HERE

18"

12"

FULLY BAKED

12 SLICES

2"

3"

ROLLED OUT DOUGH

ROLLED UP DOUGH

PROJECT: *ENTENMANN'S L.F. CINN. RAIS. SWEET ROLL*

NUTRITION STATS: *FAT-2G/CAL.-160*   JOB NO. *ELF359972-CRSR*

TOP SECRET RECIPES VERSION OF

ENTENMANN'S LIGHT LOW-FAT GOURMET CINNAMON ROLLS

☆　　　✌　　　✴　　　✎　　　☺　　　✂　　　☞

You say you like your cinnamon rolls oversize? Then this is the clone recipe for you. You'll find this method is very similar to the previous recipe, but it makes rolls almost twice the size, and there ain't no raisins. Otherwise, the recipe still uses the same filling formula, with Wondra flour to keep it from liquefying. And like the other recipe, the icing here includes our good friend, fat-free cream cheese, to create a smooth consistency while keeping the goopy fat grams at bay.

ROLLS

2 teaspoons yeast
½ cup warm water
¼ cup sugar
1⅔ cups bread flour

½ teaspoon baking powder
¼ teaspoon salt
2 tablespoons shortening, melted
3 tablespoons egg substitute

FILLING

¼ cup fat-free butter-flavored
　　spread
⅓ cup light brown sugar

2 tablespoons Wondra flour
2 teaspoons cinnamon

ICING

½ cup powdered sugar
2 tablespoons fat-free cream
　　cheese

2 to 3 drops vanilla extract
dash salt

1. Dissolve the yeast in the warm water. When the yeast is dissolved, add the sugar and stir until it is dissolved as well. In about 5 minutes, foam will form on the surface. (If foam does not form, your yeast may be too old or the water may be too hot. Try again.)
2. In a large bowl, mix the flour, baking powder, and salt together.
3. Melt the shortening in the microwave, set on high, for about 1 minute. Add the melted shortening, egg substitute, and yeast mixture to the flour and stir by hand until all ingredients are combined. Use your hands to knead the dough for about 5 minutes, then form it into a ball and put it into a covered bowl in a warm spot for 1 to 1½ hours or until it doubles in size.
4. Roll dough out onto a floured surface so that it is a rectangle measuring 18 inches long and 12 inches wide.
5. Use a spatula to spread the butter-flavored spread evenly over the surface of the dough. Combine the brown sugar, Wondra flour, and cinnamon in a small bowl. Spread this mixture evenly over the surface of the dough.
6. Starting from the top edge, roll the dough down until it forms a long roll. Cut off the ends, then slice the dough into 8 even slices and arrange them, cut side down, in a 9 × 13-inch greased baking pan or dish. Cover the pan with plastic wrap and let the rolls rise again for 1 to 1½ hours in a warm place.
7. Preheat oven to 400 degrees.
8. Remove the plastic from the pan and bake the rolls for 18 to 22 minutes or until brown.
9. As rolls bake, combine the icing ingredients in a medium bowl with an electric mixer. Mix on high speed for about 1 minute.
10. When rolls are cool, spread icing over the top of each one. Cover the baking dish and store the rolls at room temperature until you are ready to serve them.

- MAKES 8 ROLLS.

• • • •

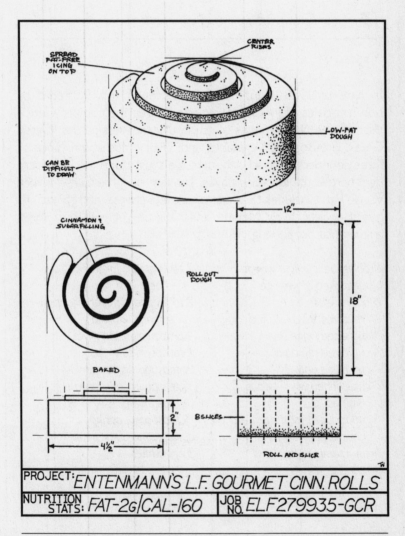

SPREAD FAT-FREE ICING ON TOP

CENTER RISES

LOW-FAT DOUGH

CAN BE DIFFICULT TO DRAW

CINNAMON & SUGAR FILLING

ROLL OUT DOUGH

12"

18"

BAKED

2"

4½"

8 SLICES

ROLL AND SLICE

PROJECT: *ENTENMANN'S L.F. GOURMET CINN. ROLLS*

NUTRITION STATS: *FAT-2G/CAL-160*

JOB NO. *ELF 279935-GCR*

TOP SECRET RECIPES
VERSION OF

GARDENBURGER CLASSIC GREEK VEGGIE PATTY

☆   ✄   💣   ✎   ☯   ✂   ☞

In June of 1998, Gardenburger was on a roll. Bolstered by booming sales of its Original Veggie Burger, the company introduced three new varieties of its popular meatless patties: Classic Greek, Fire-Roasted Vegetable, and Savory Mushroom. Since all three sounded so good, I thought we'd just clone the lot of 'em right here in the following pages. The first one, the Classic Greek Veggie Patty, includes calamata olives, feta cheese, and spinach to give it a distinctively Mediterranean flavor, yet with only three grams of fat per serving.

2 tablespoons bulgur wheat
1 cup cooked brown rice
½ pound white button
   mushrooms, quartered
⅔ cup diced white onion
¼ cup diced red onion
½ cup rolled oats
¼ cup canned white beans,
   drained
⅔ cup reduced-fat mozzarella
   cheese (2% fat)
¼ cup crumbled feta
   cheese

2 tablespoons fat-free cottage
   cheese
2 tablespoons frozen chopped
   spinach, thawed
4 pitted calamata olives
1 teaspoon salt
½ teaspoon onion powder
½ teaspoon garlic powder
¼ teaspoon parsley
¼ teaspoon paprika
dash ground black pepper
3 egg whites
2 tablespoons cornstarch

1. Add ¼ cup of boiling water to the bulgur wheat in a small bowl or measuring cup and let it sit for about 1 hour. Now is a good time to prepare the brown rice according to the directions on the package.
2. Steam the quartered mushrooms for 10 minutes or until tender. Remove the mushrooms from your steamer, and replace them with the onions. Steam the diced onions for 10 minutes or until the pieces become translucent. Keep the steamed mushrooms and onions separate and set them aside.
3. Add ½ cup of water to the rolled oats and let them soak for at least 10 minutes, until soft.
4. Drain any excess water from the bulgur wheat and oats, then combine the grains with the steamed mushrooms, rice, beans, cheeses, spinach, olives, and spices in a food processor and pulse 3 to 4 times until the ingredients are chopped but not pureed. You want a coarse texture with some identifiable chunks of grain, mushrooms, beans, cheese, and olives.
5. Pour the mixture into a bowl with the remaining ingredients and mix well.
6. Preheat the oven to 300 degrees and set a large skillet over medium/low heat.
7. Spray the skillet with a light coating of olive oil cooking spray. Measure ½ cup at a time of the patty mixture into the pan and shape with a spoon into a 3¾-inch patty that is approximately ½ inch thick. Cook the patties in batches for 2 to 4 minutes per side, or until light brown on the surface.
8. When all of the patties have been cooked in the skillet, arrange them on a lightly sprayed baking sheet and bake for 20 to 25 minutes in the oven. Be sure to turn them over halfway through the cooking time. You can serve the patties immediately or freeze them, like the original, when they have cooled.
9. If you freeze the patties, you can reheat them several ways. Simply spray a light coating of olive oil cooking spray on each side and heat each patty in a pan over medium heat for 3 to 4 minutes per side until it is hot in the center. You can also use a grill to prepare the patties. Just be sure to spray each frozen patty with the oil, and be sure the flames are low. Cook for

3 to 4 minutes per side. Those are the best cooking methods; however, you can also prepare a frozen patty by microwaving it for 30 to 35 seconds, then turn the patty over and zap it for another 30 to 35 seconds. Finally, you can heat a frozen patty in the microwave for 30 to 35 seconds, then place the partially defrosted patty in a toaster or toaster oven and cook it on medium heat until it's hot in the center.

- MAKES 8 PATTIES.

Nutrition Facts

SERVING SIZE—1 PATTY	FAT (PER SERVING)—3 G
TOTAL SERVINGS—8	CALORIES (PER SERVING)—150

• • • •

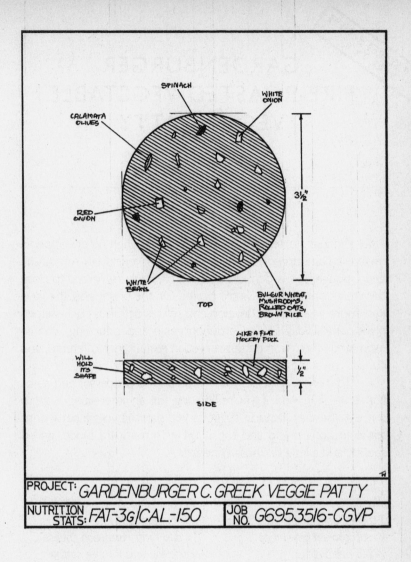

SPINACH

WHITE
ONION

CALAMATA
OLIVES

3½"

RED
ONION

WHITE
BEANS

BULGUR WHEAT,
MUSHROOMS,
ROLLED OATS,
BROWN RICE

TOP

LIKE A FLAT
HOCKEY PUCK

WILL
HOLD
ITS
SHAPE

½"

SIDE

PROJECT: *GARDENBURGER C. GREEK VEGGIE PATTY*

NUTRITION STATS: *FAT-3g/CAL.-150*

JOB NO. *G6953516-CGVP*

GARDENBURGER FIRE-ROASTED VEGETABLE VEGGIE PATTY

Paul Wenner started his company in 1985 when he developed a meatless hamburger from leftovers at his vegetarian restaurant. Even though his Gardenburger was a hit, Paul was forced to close the restaurant due to dwindling sales. On the bright side, this gave Paul more free time to develop and sell his delicious puck-shaped plant patty. Today, Paul's Gardenburger brand is thriving, with an estimated fifty million patties served in restaurants, cafeterias, and concession stands in 1998 alone.

To make this clone, you'll need a food processor and a hot barbecue grill. And if you're looking for an interesting way to serve it, the manufacturer suggests you slap the veggie patty onto some focaccia bread and top it off with marinara sauce, grilled squash, and a little Parmesan cheese.

1 head garlic
olive oil
2 tablespoons bulgur wheat
2/3 cup cooked brown rice
1/4 red bell pepper
1 ear yellow sweet corn
1/4 red onion
1/2 small tomato
1 pound white button mushrooms, quartered
1 cup diced white onion

1/2 cup rolled oats
2/3 cup reduced-fat mozzarella cheese (2% fat)
1/4 cup Kraft Parmesan cheese
2 tablespoons fat-free cottage cheese
1 1/4 teaspoons salt
1/2 teaspoon garlic powder
1/2 teaspoon paprika
1/2 teaspoon onion powder
dash ground black pepper

2 egg whites
3 tablespoons cornstarch
2 tablespoons cornmeal
2 teaspoons minced sun-dried
    tomatoes (marinated and
    drained)

2 teaspoons lemon juice
2 teaspoons juice from
    canned jalapeños
    (nacho slices)

1. Preheat your oven to 325 degrees.
2. To roast the garlic, cut about ½ inch off the top of the garlic head. Cut the roots so that the garlic will sit flat. Remove most of the papery skin from the garlic, but leave enough so that the cloves stay together. Place the head of garlic in a small casserole dish or baking pan, drizzle about a tablespoon of olive oil over it, and cover it with a lid or foil. Bake for 1 hour. Remove the garlic from the oven and let it cool until you can handle it.
3. Add ¼ cup of boiling water to the bulgur wheat in a small bowl or measuring cup and let it sit for about 1 hour. Prepare the brown rice according to the directions on the package.
4. To fire-roast the vegetables, use a barbecue grill preheated to medium. Rub olive oil on ¼ of a red bell pepper, an ear of corn, ¼ of a red onion, and ½ of a small tomato. Place the vegetables on the hot grill with the skin of the pepper and tomato facing toward the flame. Turn the corn and red onion as they cook. Grill for 30 minutes or until vegetables are tender. The skin of the red bell pepper should turn black so that it can be quickly peeled off. Also remove the skin from the tomato. (If you don't have a grill, you can roast the vegetables in your oven set to high broil for around 15 to 20 minutes. Face the skin of the tomato and pepper toward the heat and be sure to turn the corn and red onion as they cook.) Dice the pepper, onion, and tomato when cool. Keep separate.
5. Steam the quartered mushrooms for 10 minutes or until tender. Remove the mushrooms from your steamer and replace them with the white onion. Steam the diced onion for 10 minutes or until the pieces become translucent. Keep these two ingredients separate and set aside.

6. Add ½ cup of water to the rolled oats and let them soak for at least 10 minutes, until soft.

7. Drain any excess water from the bulgur wheat and oats, then combine the grains with the steamed mushrooms, rice, cheeses, corn, and spices in a food processor and pulse 4 or 5 times until the ingredients are chopped but not pureed. You want a coarse texture with some identifiable chunks of grain, mushrooms, corn, and cheese.

8. Pour the mixture into a bowl with the remaining ingredients and mix well.

9. Preheat the oven to 300 degrees and set a large skillet over medium/low heat.

10. Spray the skillet with a light coating of olive oil cooking spray. Measure ½ cup at a time of the patty mixture into the pan and shape with a spoon into a 3¾-inch patty that is approximately ½ inch thick. Cook the patties in batches for 2 to 4 minutes per side, or until light brown on the surface.

11. When all of the patties have been cooked in the skillet, arrange them on a lightly sprayed baking sheet and bake for 20 to 25 minutes in the oven. Be sure to turn them over halfway through the cooking time. You can serve the patties immediately or freeze them, like the originals, when they have cooled.

12. If you freeze the patties like the originals, you can reheat them several ways. Refer to step #9 on page 37 for heating instructions.

- MAKES 8 PATTIES.

Nutrition Facts

SERVING SIZE—1 PATTY	FAT (PER SERVING)—3 G
TOTAL SERVINGS—8	CALORIES (PER SERVING)—150

• • • •

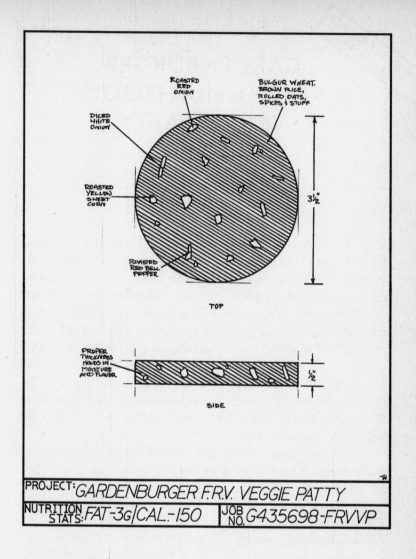

ROASTED RED ONION

BULGUR WHEAT, BROWN RICE, ROLLED OATS, SPICES & STUFF

DICED WHITE ONION

ROASTED YELLOW SWEET CORN

3½"

ROASTED RED BELL PEPPER

TOP

PROPER THICKNESS HOLDS IN MOISTURE AND FLAVOR

½"

SIDE

PROJECT: GARDENBURGER F.R.V. VEGGIE PATTY

NUTRITION STATS: FAT -3g / CAL. -150   JOB NO. G435698-FRVVP

43

TOP SECRET RECIPES
VERSION OF

GARDENBURGER
SAVORY MUSHROOM
VEGGIE PATTY

☆   ✄   ●   ✎   ◉   ✂   ☞

Chef Paul Wenner fathered a hot product when he ground up those leftover vegetables at his restaurant and formed them into the shape of a hamburger patty. When Paul got out of the restaurant business, he peddled the meatless patties out of his van under the name Wholesome & Hearty Foods. In 1992, when his company went public, the stock shot up to $30 from $3 on rumors that McDonald's was planning to sell the veggie patties under the golden arches. When those rumors proved to be false, the stock came crashing down quicker than sales figures for the McLean Deluxe. Later, the name of the company was changed to Gardenburger, and new products, such as the Savory Mushroom Veggie Patty, were developed.

For this clone, you'll need to track down three types of mushrooms: the common white button, brown (or crimini), and portobello. You'll also need a food processor to mash everything up real good.

2 tablespoons bulgur wheat
⅔ cup cooked brown rice
6 ounces white button
    mushrooms, quartered
6 ounces brown Italian mushrooms
    (crimini), quartered
4 ounces portobello mushroom
    (1 small cap), quartered

1 cup diced white onion
    (about ½ cup steamed)
½ cup rolled oats
⅔ cup reduced-fat
    mozzarella cheese
    (2% fat)
2 tablespoons shredded
    Gorgonzola cheese

2 tablespoons fat-free cottage
   cheese
1 ¼ teaspoons salt
1 teaspoon onion powder
½ teaspoon garlic powder
dash ground black pepper

2 egg whites
3 tablespoons cornstarch
1 tablespoon all-purpose flour
2 teaspoons soy sauce
2 teaspoons brown sugar
2 teaspoons molasses

1. Add ¼ cup of boiling water to the bulgur wheat in a small bowl or measuring cup and let it sit for about 1 hour. Prepare the brown rice according to the directions on the package.

2. Steam the quartered mushrooms for 10 minutes or until tender. Remove the mushrooms from your steamer and replace them with the onion. Steam the diced onion for 10 minutes or until the pieces become translucent. Keep the mushrooms separate from the onions and set them aside.

3. Add ½ cup of water to the rolled oats and let them soak for at least 10 minutes, until soft.

4. Drain any excess water from the bulgur wheat and oats, then combine the grains with the steamed mushrooms, rice, cheeses, and spices in a food processor and pulse 4 or 5 times until the ingredients are chopped but not pureed. You want a coarse texture with some identifiable chunks of grain, mushrooms, and cheese.

5. Pour the mixture into a bowl with the remaining ingredients and mix well.

6. Preheat the oven to 300 degrees and set a large skillet over medium/low heat.

7. Spray the skillet with a light coating of olive oil cooking spray. Measure ½ cup of the patty mixture at a time into the pan and shape with a spoon into a 3¾-inch patty that is approximately ½ inch thick. Cook the patties in batches for 2 to 4 minutes per side or until light brown on the surface.

8. When all of the patties have been cooked in the skillet, arrange them on a lightly sprayed baking sheet and bake for 20 to 25 minutes in the oven. Be sure to turn them over halfway through the cooking time. You can serve the patties immediately or freeze them, like the originals, when they have cooled.

9. If you freeze the patties, you can reheat them several ways. Refer to step #9 on page 37 for heating instructions.

• MAKES 8 PATTIES.

Nutrition Facts

SERVING SIZE—1 PATTY	FAT (PER SERVING)—3 G
TOTAL SERVINGS—8	CALORIES (PER SERVING)—140

• • • •

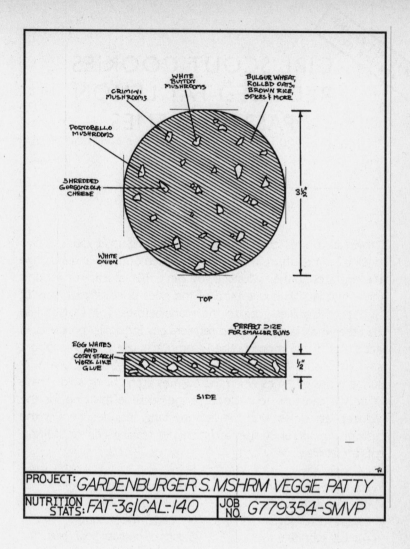

CRIMINI
MUSHROOMS

WHITE
BUTTON
MUSHROOMS

BULGUR WHEAT,
ROLLED OATS,
BROWN RICE,
SPICES & MORE

PORTOBELLO
MUSHROOMS

3½"

SHREDDED
GORGONZOLA
CHEESE

WHITE
ONION

TOP

PERFECT SIZE
FOR SMALLER BUNS

EGG WHITES
AND
CORN STARCH
WORK LIKE
GLUE

½"

SIDE

PROJECT: GARDENBURGER S. MSHRM VEGGIE PATTY

NUTRITION STATS: FAT-3g/CAL-140   **JOB NO.** G779354-SMVP

GIRL SCOUT COOKIES
REDUCED-FAT LEMON
PASTRY CREMES

How can you resist the cute little girls smiling up at you with two missing front teeth, in those adorable green outfits—and a change machine around their waists? If you can't, then at least it's good to know that less than one-third of the sales price of each box of Girl Scout Cookies goes to the manufacturer. That's much less than the wholesale price food retailers pay for similar products. In fact, most of the money raised from each sale goes to support the Girl Scouts. But how do we get our Girl Scout Cookie fix during those off times when the cookies aren't being sold? That's when we can turn to a clone recipe such as this one for the reduced-fat cookie with the lemony tang. Included here is the custom Top Secret Recipes technique for making a delicious filling, entirely fat-free.

⅓ cup shortening
⅓ cup granulated sugar
½ cup powdered sugar
¼ cup egg substitute
½ teaspoon salt
½ teaspoon lemon extract

¾ teaspoon baking soda
⅓ cup plus 1 tablespoon
   buttermilk (1% fat)
3 cups all-purpose flour (plus
   about ¼ cup reserved for
   rolling the dough)

GLAZE
½ cup powdered sugar

2½ teaspoons water

FILLING

1 cup granulated sugar	1/8 teaspoon salt
1/4 cup very hot water	2 drops yellow food coloring
1/4 teaspoon lemon extract	1 cup sifted powdered sugar

1. To make the cookies, cream together the first 7 ingredients (shortening through baking soda) in a large bowl with an electric mixer. Add the buttermilk and mix until incorporated.

2. Add the 3 cups of flour to the wet mixture, 1 cup at a time. Use your hands to form the dough into a ball, then cover it with plastic wrap and chill for 1 hour.

3. Preheat oven to 325 degrees.

4. Roll dough out onto a lightly floured surface to about 1/16 inch thick. Punch out cookies with a 1 1/2-inch cutter and arrange them on an ungreased cookie sheet. Bake for 8 to 12 minutes or until just turning light brown around the edges. Turn pan around halfway through cooking time to help the cookies bake evenly.

5. As cookies bake, prepare glaze by combining powdered sugar and water in a small bowl. Mix until smooth. Cover and set aside.

6. When cookies have cooled, dip a brush in the glaze, wipe off excess, and brush a very, very light coating of the glaze over the top of each cookie.

7. Prepare the filling by combining the granulated sugar, hot water, lemon extract, salt, and yellow food coloring in a microwave-safe medium bowl (glass or ceramic works the best). Stir the mixture for at least 30 seconds to begin dissolving the sugar.

8. Cover the bowl with plastic wrap, and then microwave mixture for 2 minutes at 50% power. Remove mixture from microwave and stir very gently to help dissolve the sugar crystals around the sides and bottom of the bowl. Cover the bowl again, then microwave mixture at full power for 2 more minutes. Remove the bowl from the microwave. Poke holes in the plastic wrap to let the steam escape. Let mixture cool for 15 minutes. Do not let mixture sit longer than this or

a hardened skin may develop and new sugar crystals may form.

9. After mixture has cooled for 15 minutes, stir it again very gently to dissolve any additional crystals that may have formed, and then add 1 cup of powdered sugar. Stir very gently to incorporate the sugar until mixture is smooth. Cover mixture again until it can be handled.

10. Roll filling into ½-inch balls and flatten between two cookies, with the frosted sides facing out. Repeat with the remaining filling.

- MAKES 42 SANDWICH COOKIES.

Nutrition Facts

SERVING SIZE—3 COOKIES	FAT (PER SERVING)—4.5 G
TOTAL SERVINGS—14	CALORIES (PER SERVING)—150

• ⟩ • •

TOP SECRET RECIPES VERSION OF

HEALTHY CHOICE TRADITIONAL PASTA SAUCE

It was a heart attack that inspired Charles M. Harper of ConAgra Foods to come up with a new product line. In 1988, the Healthy Choice brand introduced frozen dinners with reduced fat, sodium, and cholesterol. Hundreds of other products followed through the '90s, including this fat-free pasta sauce, which hit stores in 1992. It's a cinch to make and goes great on any pasta, pizza, or meatball sandwich. If it's a chunky sauce you're looking for, check out the next recipe.

2 10¾-ounce cans tomato puree
1 cup water
½ teaspoon dried minced garlic
1 teaspoon dried minced onion
5 teaspoons granulated sugar
½ teaspoon salt

1 tablespoon lemon juice
¼ teaspoon dried parsley
⅛ teaspoon dried thyme
¼ teaspoon dried basil
¼ teaspoon dried oregano
dash ground black pepper

1. Combine all of the ingredients in a medium saucepan over medium/high heat and bring to a boil.
2. Reduce heat to low and simmer for 1 to 1½ hours or until sauce is thick.

• MAKES 2½ CUPS.

Nutrition Facts
SERVING SIZE—½ CUP
TOTAL SERVINGS—5

FAT (PER SERVING)—0 G
CALORIES (PER SERVING)—50

• • • •

TOP SECRET RECIPES
VERSION OF

HEALTHY CHOICE CHUNKY TOMATO, MUSHROOM & GARLIC PASTA SAUCE

Healthy Choice was one of the first low-fat brands to hit the stores. The *Wall Street Journal* reported in 1993, "When Healthy Choice dinners first arrived in stores, big competitors were caught off guard: nothing quite like it had ever been marketed on a large scale." But nowadays the competition ain't so lean. You'll find more than a dozen brands devoted to the same low-fat, healthy claims in stores, all fighting it out for shelf space and market share.

If you like your marinara sauce with big chunks of veggies in it, then this is the one you'll want to make. The canned tomatoes, plus fresh mushrooms, onion, and garlic make for a thicker sauce that works great over your favorite pasta creation.

2 10¾-ounce cans tomato
    puree
1 cup water
1 cup chopped canned
    tomatoes
¾ cup sliced white button
    mushrooms
2 teaspoons minced garlic
¼ cup minced white onion

5 teaspoons granulated
    sugar
½ teaspoon salt
4 teaspoons lemon juice
¼ teaspoon dried parsley
⅛ teaspoon dried thyme
¼ teaspoon dried basil
¼ teaspoon dried oregano
dash ground black pepper

1. Combine all of the ingredients in a medium saucepan over medium/high heat and bring to a boil.
2. Reduce heat to low and simmer for 1 to 1½ hours or until sauce is thick.

- MAKES 2½ CUPS.

Nutrition Facts

SERVING SIZE—½ CUP   FAT (PER SERVING)—0 G
TOTAL SERVINGS—5   CALORIES (PER SERVING)—45

•   •   •   •

TOP SECRET RECIPES
VERSION OF

KEEBLER REDUCED-FAT PECAN SANDIES

☆   ✂   ✦   ✎   ◐   ✂   ☞

The full-fat version of these delicious discs are the top-selling shortbread cookies in the United States. It's no wonder the baked-goods giant elected to introduce a reduced-fat version in 1994. You'll find this clone as easy to make as any other cookie recipe, but with much less fat in the crispy finished product.

⅓ cup shortening
1 cup powdered sugar
½ teaspoon baking soda
½ teaspoon vanilla
¼ teaspoon salt

⅛ teaspoon coconut extract
2 tablespoons buttermilk
1½ cups sifted all-purpose flour
¼ teaspoon baking powder
¼ cup finely chopped pecans

1. Preheat oven to 325 degrees.
2. With an electric mixer, cream together the shortening, sugar, baking soda, vanilla, salt, coconut extract, and buttermilk in a large bowl.
3. Combine flour and baking powder in another bowl.
4. Pour the dry ingredients into the wet ingredients and mix well.
5. Add pecans and mix until incorporated.
6. Roll dough into 1-inch balls and press them down onto an ungreased cookie sheet. Flatten the dough slightly with your fingers, and bake for 15 to 18 minutes or until cookies are light brown.

• MAKES 30 COOKIES.

SERVING SIZE—1 COOKIE   FAT (PER SERVING)—3 G

TOTAL SERVINGS—30   CALORIES (PER SERVING)—80

• • • • •

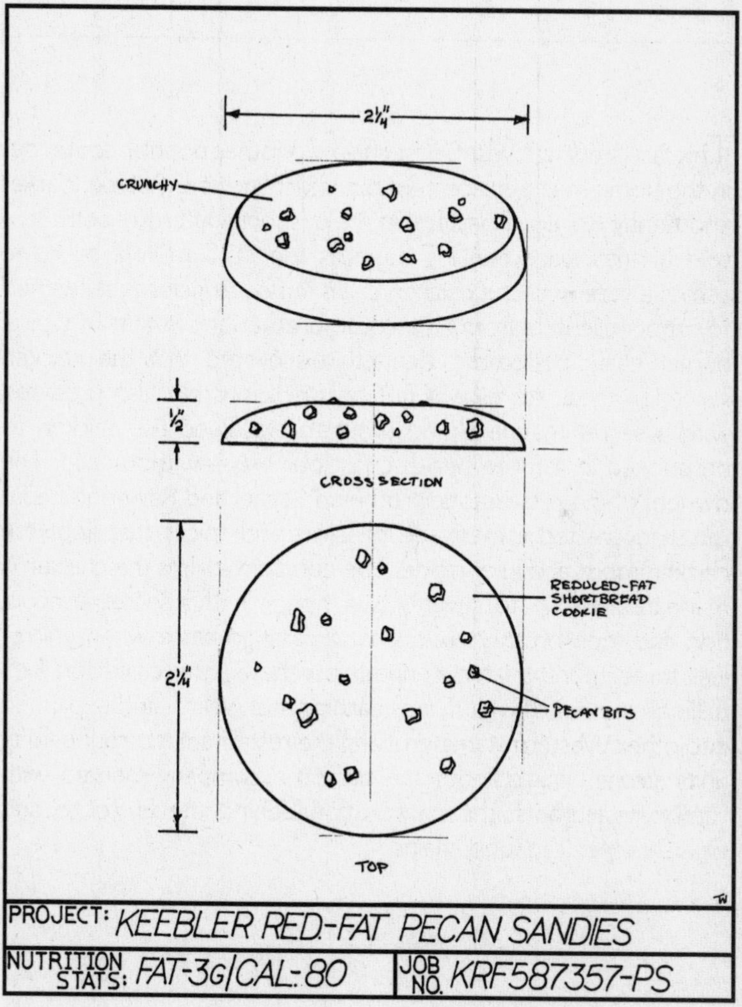

2¼"

CRUNCHY

½

CROSS SECTION

2¼"

REDUCED-FAT
SHORTBREAD
COOKIE

PECAN BITS

TOP

PROJECT: KEEBLER RED.-FAT PECAN SANDIES

NUTRITION STATS: FAT-3G/CAL-80   JOB NO. KRF587357-PS

TOP SECRET RECIPES
VERSION OF

KOO KOO ROO
ORIGINAL SKINLESS
FLAME-BROILED CHICKEN

This fast-growing West Coast chain is another popular contender in the home meal replacement biz, which includes Boston Market and Kenny Rogers' Roasters. In 1990, shortly after Kenneth Berg sold his mortgage banking business for $125 million, he came across a little two-unit chicken chain in Los Angeles that seemed to attract clientele from an income bracket above that of typical burger chain customers. Kenneth discovered that the chicken served in these stores was not only delicious but also prepared with a secret marinade and baste that allowed the chicken to be cooked in a more health-conscious way—without skin. The owners of the restaurants, brothers Michael and Raymond Bada-lian, had created a marinade of juices and spices that kept the chicken moist and juicy inside. The company claims the chicken is marinated for up to seventy-two hours in this secret concoction and then brushed with a tangy orange baste when grilling. Just three months later, Kenneth purchased the chain for $2.5 million—ten times what it was earning each year—and expanded into other Western states, growing the restaurant to around forty units strong. That's about the time the company merged with Family Restaurants, the corporation behind the El Torito and Chi-Chi's Mexican food chains.

MARINADE

I cup water
I cup apple juice
I cup V-8 juice
I tablespoon lemon juice

½ cup pineapple juice
I cup chopped onion
2 teaspoons salt
2 teaspoons ground black pepper

I whole chicken, skinned and cut
 into 8 pieces (legs, thighs,
 breasts, and wings)

BASTE

2 tablespoons plus I teaspoon
 vegetable oil
½ cup thinly sliced onions
I 10¾-ounce can tomato puree
¼ cup water

I tablespoon white vinegar
I tablespoon lemon juice
¼ teaspoon salt
dash ground black pepper
dash garlic powder

1. Combine all of the ingredients for the marinade in a medium bowl. Mix well.
2. Add chicken to the marinade and leave it for at least 24 hours. It is even better if you let the chicken marinate longer, for as much as 48 to 72 hours.
3. Sometime before the chicken is done marinating, prepare the basting sauce by heating I teaspoon of the oil in a medium skillet. Sauté the sliced onions until they begin to blacken a bit. Pour the onions into a medium saucepan with the other baste ingredients. Bring mixture to a full boil, then reduce heat and simmer for 5 to 7 minutes. Remove from heat. When cool, cover the baste and chill it until it's needed.
4. When you are ready to cook the chicken, fire up your grill to medium heat. Grill the chicken for 5 to 6 minutes, then turn it over and grill for another 5 to 6 minutes. Turn chicken over once more and brush the top with the baste. Grill for another 5 to 6 minutes, then turn the chicken over again, baste the other side, and cook it until it's done—around 25 to 35 min-

utes total cooking time. You should see a few charred black spots on the surface of the chicken, but don't let it burn.

- SERVES 4.

Nutrition Facts

SERVING SIZE—2 PIECES   FAT (PER SERVING)—8 G

TOTAL SERVINGS—4   CALORIES (PER SERVING)—195

• • • •

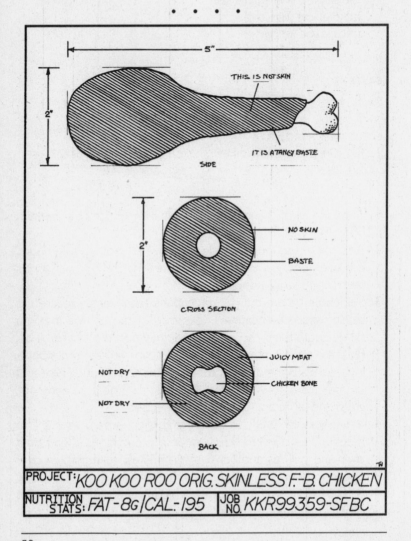

PROJECT: *KOO KOO ROO ORIG. SKINLESS F.-B. CHICKEN*

NUTRITION STATS: *FAT-8G/CAL.-195*   JOB NO. *KKR99359-SFBC*

TOP SECRET RECIPES
VERSION OF

KOO KOO ROO
SANTA FE PASTA

☆   ✌   💣   ✒   🎱   ✂   ☞

In 1998, ex–Chrysler chairman Lee Iacocca took the reins at the struggling chicken chain. Lee had been an investor in the company since 1995, so when increasing competition from chains like Boston Market and Kenny Rogers' Roasters caused the Koo Koo Roo bottom line to sag, he was called in to rescue it. Can Lee perform the same comeback magic as he did with Chrysler's historic turnaround in the early '80s? While we wait to find out, let's make some pasta. This one goes great with the chicken from the previous recipe or with just about any other meal. The Southwestern-style dressing includes a small amount of oil, but the total fat grams per six-ounce serving stays quite modest.

1 16-ounce package rotini pasta	4 to 5 quarts water

DRESSING

1 cup V-8 juice	½ teaspoon paprika
2 tablespoons olive oil	¾ teaspoon salt
4 teaspoons red wine vinegar	¼ teaspoon ground black pepper
1 teaspoon chili powder	⅛ teaspoon garlic powder

⅔ cup grated Parmesan cheese	2 tablespoons diced red bell pepper
½ cup cooked yellow corn kernels	
¼ cup chopped fresh cilantro	2 tablespoons diced green bell pepper
¼ cup chopped green onion	

1 boneless chicken breast fillet, cooked and diced (best to use chicken breast meat from page 56)

1. Prepare the pasta by bringing 4 to 5 quarts of water to a rolling boil in a large saucepan. Add pasta to the pan, and when water begins to boil again, cook for 8 to 11 minutes. Pasta should be *al dente*, or mostly tender but with a slight toughness in the middle.
2. Whisk all of the dressing ingredients together in a small bowl. Cover and chill the dressing until you're ready to use it.
3. When pasta is done, drain it and pour it into a large bowl to cool. Add the dressing, then toss.
4. Add the remaining ingredients to the pasta and toss until pasta is well coated. Cover and chill for several hours before serving.

• SERVES 10 AS A SIDE DISH.

Nutrition Facts

SERVING SIZE—6 OUNCES   FAT (PER SERVING)—5 G

TOTAL SERVINGS—10   CALORIES (PER SERVING)—230

• • • •

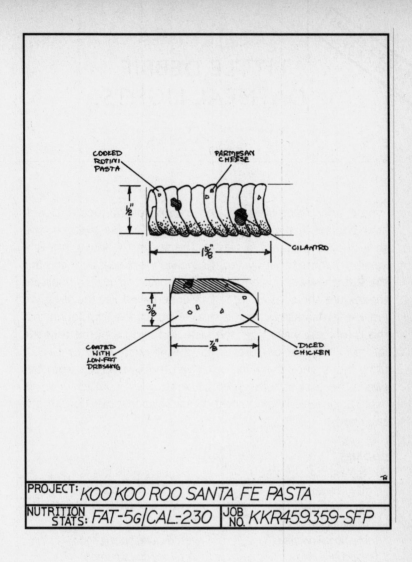

COOKED
ROTINI
PASTA

PARMESAN
CHEESE

½"

1⅝"

CILANTRO

⅜"

⅞"

COATED
WITH
LOW-FAT
DRESSING

DICED
CHICKEN

TW

PROJECT: *KOO KOO ROO SANTA FE PASTA*

NUTRITION STATS: *FAT-5g/CAL-230*   **JOB NO.** *KKR459359-SFP*

61

TOP SECRET RECIPES
VERSION OF

LITTLE DEBBIE
OATMEAL LIGHTS

☆   ✄   ✒   ❂   ✂   ☞

These soft, creme-filled cookies are one of the most drooled-over goodies in the popular line of Little Debbie snacks. Good thing they're wrapped in plastic. The secret to cloning the light version of these mouthwatering sandwich cookies is in re-creating the soft, chewy consistency of the oatmeal cookies. To duplicate the texture, the cookies are slightly underbaked. For the filling, we just use marshmallow creme straight out of the jar. I found that this is the best way to get the taste and texture of the original's fat-free filling. Just be sure to eat these within a day or two of filling them, since the filling will begin to slowly creep from between the cookies. Also, keep these sandwich cookies wrapped in plastic or sealed in an airtight container so that they'll stay moist and chewy.

COOKIES

3½ tablespoons softened
    margarine
¾ cup dark brown sugar
¼ cup granulated sugar
1 tablespoon molasses
1 teaspoon vanilla

½ cup egg substitute
1½ cups all-purpose flour
1¼ cups 1-minute Quaker Oats
¾ teaspoon salt
½ teaspoon baking soda
¼ teaspoon cinnamon

1 7-ounce jar marshmallow creme

1. Preheat oven to 350 degrees.
2. In a large bowl, cream together margarine, sugars, molasses, vanilla, and egg substitute with an electric mixer.

3. In a separate bowl, combine the flour, oats, salt, baking soda, and cinnamon.
4. Combine the dry ingredients with the wet ingredients and mix by hand.
5. Drop the dough by tablespoonfuls onto a well-greased baking sheet. The dough will be very tacky, so you may wish to moisten your fingers so that the dough does not stick. With moistened fingers, press down on the dough and form it into circles about ⅛ inch thick. The circles should be about 2 inches in diameter before baking. Bake for 6 to 8 minutes or until a couple of the cookies start to darken around the edges. They will still be very tender in the center until cool. Be careful not to overcook. When cooled, the cookies should be about ¼ inch thick and very soft and chewy.
6. When the cookies have completely cooled, assemble each creme pie by spreading about 1½ tablespoons of marshmallow creme over the flat side of a cookie and press another cookie on top, making a sandwich. Repeat for the remaining cookies and filling.

- MAKES 20 SANDWICH COOKIES.

Nutrition Facts

SERVING SIZE—1 SANDWICH COOKIE

TOTAL SERVINGS—20

FAT (PER SERVING)—2.5 G

CALORIES (PER SERVING)—146

• • • •

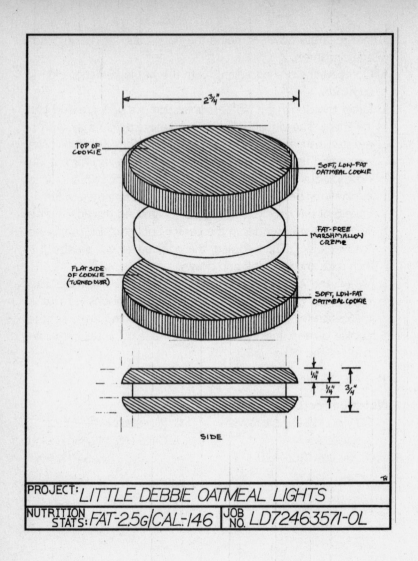

2³⁄₄"

TOP OF
COOKIE

SOFT, LOW-FAT
OATMEAL COOKIE

FAT-FREE
MARSHMALLOW
CREME

FLAT SIDE
OF COOKIE
(TURNED OVER)

SOFT, LOW-FAT
OATMEAL COOKIE

¼"

¼"

¾"

SIDE

PROJECT:	*LITTLE DEBBIE OATMEAL LIGHTS*	
NUTRITION STATS:	*FAT-2.5g/CAL.-146*	JOB NO. *LD72463571-OL*

NABISCO HONEY MAID GRAHAMS

TOP SECRET RECIPES VERSION OF

☆　　✌　　💣　　✒　　☯　　✂　　☞

The beginning of the graham cracker goes back to the early 1800s when Sylvester Graham thought his new invention was the secret to a lifetime of perfect health, even sexual prowess—certainly extraordinary claims for a cracker. But this came from the man thought to be quite a whacko in his time, since he had earlier claimed that eating ketchup could ruin your brain. So, while his crispy whole wheat creation was not the cure for every known ailment, the sweet crackers still became quite a fad, first in New England around the 1830s and then spreading across the country. Today, graham crackers remain popular as a low-fat, snack time munchable, and they're the main ingredient in s'mores.

You don't need to use graham flour for this recipe, since it's similar to the whole wheat flour you find in your local super-market. Just pick your favorite variety among these three clones of Nabisco's most popular crackers, and be sure to roll out the dough paper thin.

HONEY (ORIGINAL)

⅓ cup shortening
¾ cup plus 1 tablespoon
   granulated sugar
3 tablespoons honey, warmed
1½ teaspoons vanilla
1¾ cups whole wheat flour

1¼ cups all-purpose flour
1¼ teaspoons salt
1 teaspoon baking powder
½ teaspoon baking soda
½ cup plus 2 tablespoons water

1. Preheat oven to 300 degrees.
2. Combine shortening with sugar, honey (warmed for 20 to 30 seconds in the microwave), and vanilla in a large bowl. Blend with an electric mixer until smooth.
3. Combine flours, salt, baking powder, and baking soda in another large bowl, and then add the dry mixture to the wet ingredients and blend well with an electric mixer.
4. Slowly add the water to the mixture while beating. You may have to mix by hand until the mixture forms a large ball of dough.
5. Divide the dough in thirds and roll ⅓ out in the shape of a rectangle that is at least 1/16 inch thick on wax paper. This dough should be paper thin! It will double when cooked to the desired ⅛-inch thickness. Use a knife to trim the dough so that it has straight edges in the shape of a rectangle slightly smaller than the size of the baking sheet you are using.
6. Grease the baking sheet with a light coating of shortening. Turn the dough over onto the baking sheet, and carefully peel away the wax paper.
7. Use a knife to score the dough in 5 × 2⅜-inch rectangles. Use a toothpick to poke holes that are ¼ inch apart across the entire surface of the dough.
8. Bake for 22 to 24 minutes or until the dough begins to turn light brown around the edges. Be sure to turn the baking sheet around about halfway through the cooking time.
9. Cool the graham cracker sheets before breaking them apart along the scored lines. Repeat the process with the remaining dough.

• MAKES 44 CRACKERS.

CINNAMON

⅓ cup shortening
¾ cup plus 1 tablespoon granulated sugar
2 tablespoons honey, warmed
1 tablespoon molasses
1½ teaspoons vanilla

1¾ cups whole wheat flour
1¼ cups all-purpose flour
1¼ teaspoons salt
1 teaspoon baking powder
½ teaspoon baking soda
½ cup plus 2 tablespoons water

TOPPING

1 ½ teaspoons cinnamon   *2 tablespoons sugar*

1. Preheat oven to 300 degrees.
2. Combine shortening with sugar, honey (warmed for 20 to 30 seconds in the microwave), molasses, and vanilla in a large bowl. Blend with an electric mixer until smooth.
3. Combine flours, salt, baking powder, and baking soda in another large bowl, and then add the dry mixture to the wet ingredients and blend well with an electric mixer.
4. Slowly add the water to the mixture while beating. You may have to mix by hand until the mixture forms a large ball of dough.
5. Divide the dough in thirds and roll ⅓ out in the shape of a rectangle that is at least 1/16 inch thick on wax paper. This dough should be paper thin! It will double when cooked to the desired ⅛-inch thickness. Use a knife to trim the dough so that it has straight edges in the shape of a rectangle slightly smaller than the size of the baking sheet you are using.
6. Grease the baking sheet with a light coating of shortening. Turn the dough over onto the baking sheet, and carefully peel away the wax paper.
7. Use a knife to score the dough in 5 × 2⅜-inch rectangles. Use a toothpick to poke holes that are ¼ inch apart across the entire surface of the dough.
8. Sprinkle a light coating of the cinnamon/sugar over the top surface of the dough. Shake the baking sheet around gently to evenly distribute the cinnamon/sugar topping.
9. Bake for 22 to 24 minutes or until the dough begins to turn light brown around the edges. Be sure to turn the baking sheet around about halfway through the cooking time.
10. Cool the graham cracker sheets before breaking them apart along the scored lines. Repeat the process with the remaining dough.

- MAKES 44 CRACKERS.

CHOCOLATE

⅓ cup shortening
¾ cup plus 1 tablespoon
   granulated sugar
3 tablespoons honey, warmed
1 tablespoon chocolate syrup
1 ½ teaspoons vanilla
1 ½ cups whole wheat flour
1 ¼ cups all-purpose flour

⅓ cup cocoa
1 ¼ teaspoons salt
1 teaspoon baking powder
½ teaspoon baking soda
¼ cup water
¼ cup fat-free milk
2 tablespoons whole milk

TOPPING
2 tablespoons granulated sugar

1. Preheat oven to 300 degrees.
2. Combine shortening with sugar, honey (warmed for 20 to 30 seconds in the microwave), chocolate syrup, and vanilla in a large bowl. Blend with an electric mixer until smooth.
3. Combine flours, cocoa, salt, baking powder, and baking soda in another large bowl, and then add the dry mixture to the wet ingredients and blend well with an electric mixer.
4. Slowly add the water and milk to the mixture while beating. You may have to mix by hand until the mixture forms a large ball of dough.
5. Divide the dough in thirds and roll ⅓ out in the shape of a rectangle that is at least 1/16 inch thick on wax paper. This dough should be paper thin! It will double in thickness when cooked to the desired ⅛-inch thickness. Use a knife to trim the dough so that it has straight edges in the shape of a rectangle slightly smaller than the size of the baking sheet you are using.
6. Grease the baking sheet with a light coating of shortening. Turn the dough over onto the baking sheet and carefully peel away the wax paper.
7. Use a knife to score the dough in 5 × 2⅜-inch rectangles. Use a toothpick to poke holes that are ¼ inch apart across the entire surface of the dough.

8. Sprinkle a light coating of granulated sugar over the top surface of the dough. Gently shake the baking sheet around to help evenly distribute the sugar.
9. Bake for 22 to 24 minutes or until the dough begins to turn light brown around the edges. Be sure to turn the baking sheet around about halfway through the cooking time.
10. Cool the graham cracker sheets before breaking them apart along the scored lines. Repeat the process with the remaining dough.

• MAKES 44 CRACKERS.

Nutrition Facts

SERVING SIZE—2 CRACKERS   FAT (PER SERVING)—3 G
TOTAL SERVINGS—22   CALORIES (PER SERVING)—120

• • • •

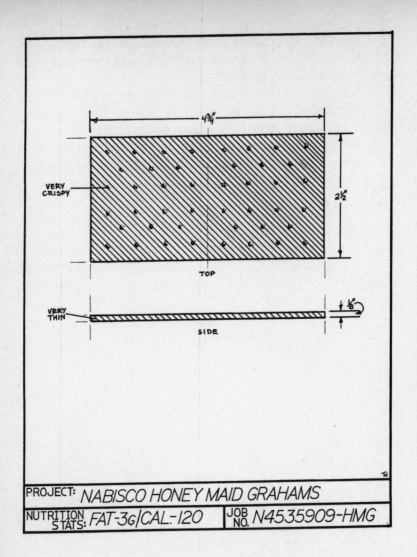

4¾"

2½"

VERY
CRISPY

TOP

VERY
THIN

SIDE

⅛"

PROJECT: NABISCO HONEY MAID GRAHAMS

NUTRITION
STATS: FAT-3g/CAL.-120   JOB
NO. N4535909-HMG

TOP SECRET RECIPES VERSION OF

NABISCO OLD FASHION GINGER SNAPS

According to legend, if you place a ginger snap in the palm of your hand and press down on the middle, and it breaks into three pieces, good luck will follow. Though you'll wish a broom would follow, since you just got crumbs all over your clean floor.

1 cup packed dark brown sugar	2 teaspoons baking soda
¾ cup granulated sugar	2 teaspoons ground ginger
6 tablespoons shortening	1 teaspoon salt
¼ cup molasses	1 teaspoon ground cinnamon
¼ cup egg substitute	½ teaspoon ground cloves
½ teaspoon vanilla	¼ cup water
2½ cups all-purpose flour	

1. Preheat oven to 300 degrees.
2. Cream together the sugars, shortening, molasses, egg substitute, and vanilla in a large bowl. Beat with an electric mixer until smooth.
3. In another large bowl, combine the flour, baking soda, ginger, salt, cinnamon, and cloves.
4. Pour the dry mixture into the wet mixture and beat while adding the water. Continue to mix until ingredients are incorporated.
5. Measure 1 rounded teaspoon of dough at a time. Roll the dough into a sphere between the palms of your hands, then press the dough onto a lightly greased cookie sheet. Flatten to about ¼ inch thick, and leave at least ½ inch between the cookies

since they will spread out a bit when baking. Use flour or water on your fingers if the dough sticks.

6. Bake cookies for 12 to 14 minutes or until edges begin to turn light brown. Cookies should be crispy, not soft, when cool.

• MAKES 120 COOKIES.

Nutrition Facts

SERVING SIZE—4 COOKIES   FAT (PER SERVING)—2.5 G

TOTAL SERVINGS—30   CALORIES (PER SERVING)—110

• • • •

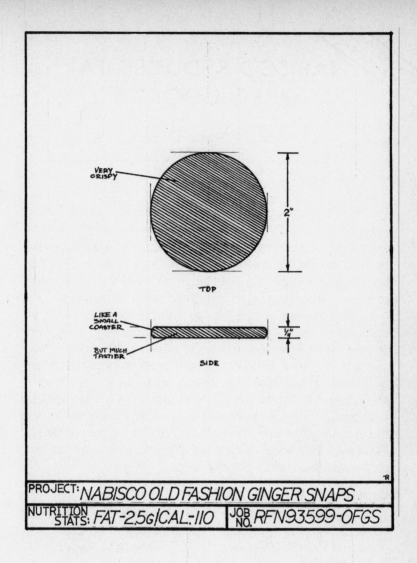

VERY
CRISPY

2"

TOP

LIKE A
SMALL
COASTER

BUT MUCH
TASTIER

SIDE

¼"

®

PROJECT: *NABISCO OLD FASHION GINGER SNAPS*

NUTRITION STATS: *FAT-2.5g/CAL.-110* JOB NO. *RFN93599-OFGS*

73

TOP SECRET RECIPES
VERSION OF

NABISCO REDUCED-FAT
OREO COOKIES

☆　　　✌︎　　　💣　　　✏️　　　☯　　　✂︎　　　☞

I've been researching the King of All Cookies for years now, and I've still not found anyone who is sure where the name *Oreo* came from. One of the most interesting and obscure explanations I've heard is that the two o's from the word *chocolate* were placed on both sides of *re* from the word *creme*. This way the name seems to mimic the construction of the famed sandwich cookie.

That may not be true, but I do know this for sure: Nabisco introduced a reduced-fat version of its popular cookie in 1994. With only half the fat, it manages to taste just as good as the original version invented way back in 1912. We cut back on the fat for our clone here by re-creating the creme filling without any of the shortening you'd find in the original full-fat version. We do this with a special technique developed in the secret underground Top Secret Recipes test kitchen that allows you to create a delicious, fat-free filling in your microwave. If you want the cookies as dark as the original, include the optional brown paste food coloring in your recipe.

COOKIES

1 18¼-ounce package reduced-fat devil's food cake mix (Betty Crocker Sweet Rewards is best)
¼ cup shortening, melted
½ cup all-purpose flour, measured then sifted

¼ cup egg substitute
3 tablespoons brown paste food coloring (2 1-ounce containers)*
3 tablespoons water

*This addition of brown paste food coloring is an optional step to help re-create the color of the original cookie. If you do not use the paste food coloring, be sure to change the amount of water added to the wafer cookies from 3 tablespoons to ⅓ cup. The food coloring gives the cookies the dark brown, almost black color. The coloring can be found with cake decorating supplies at art supply and craft stores.

FILLING

1 cup granulated sugar	dash salt
¼ cup hot water	1⅓ cups powdered sugar
½ teaspoon vanilla (clear is best)*	

1. Combine the cookie ingredients in a large bowl. Add the water a bit at a time until the dough forms. (You may need as much as ¼ cup of water to create a dough ball that is pliable and easy to roll but not sticky.) Cover and chill for 2 hours.
2. Preheat oven to 350 degrees.
3. On a floured surface, roll out a portion of the dough to just under 1/16 inch thick. To cut, use a cutter or lid from a spice container with a 1½-inch diameter (Schilling brand is good). Arrange the cut dough on a cookie sheet that is sprayed with a light coating of nonstick spray. Bake for 10 minutes. Remove the chocolate wafers from the oven and cool completely.
4. As the wafers bake, make the filling by combining the granulated sugar, hot water, vanilla, and salt in a medium bowl. Stir mixture for about 30 seconds to begin dissolving the sugar.
5. Cover bowl with plastic wrap and microwave on 50% power for 2 minutes. Remove the bowl from the microwave. Stir very gently to help dissolve the sugar crystals around the sides and bottom of the bowl. Cover bowl again and microwave at full power for 2 more minutes. Remove the bowl from the microwave, and poke holes in the plastic wrap to let the steam escape. Let the mixture cool for 15 minutes. Do not let the mixture stand for longer than this or sugar crystals may begin to form.
6. After mixture has cooled for 15 minutes, stir it very gently once again to dissolve any additional crystals that may have formed, then add the 1⅓ cups of powdered sugar. Stir gently to incorporate the sugar, until mixture is smooth. Cover mixture again until it can be handled.

*This clear vanilla can also be found with cake decorating supplies in craft stores. The clear vanilla will give you a much whiter filling like the original, although the brown vanilla works fine for taste, if that's all you've got on hand.

7. When the cookies have cooled, roll a small portion (rounded ¼ teaspoon) of the filling into a ball (just over ¼ inch in diameter), and press it between two of the cookies. Repeat with the remaining cookies.

- MAKES 54 SANDWICH COOKIES.

TIDBITS

If the dough for the wafers seems too sticky, you can work in as much as ¼ cup of additional flour as you pat out and roll the dough. Use just enough flour to make the dough workable but not tough.

Nutrition Facts

SERVING SIZE—3 COOKIES FAT (PER SERVING)—3.5 G
TOTAL SERVINGS—18 CALORIES (PER SERVING)—150

• • • •

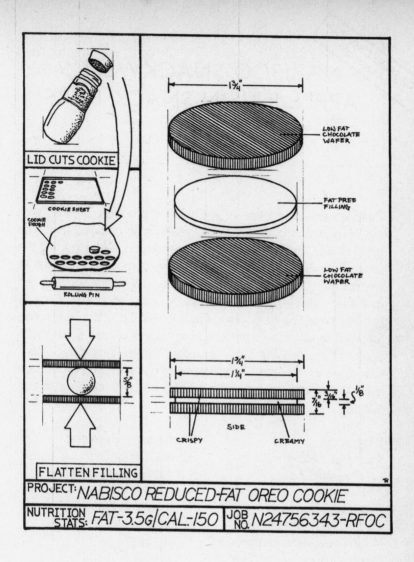

LID CUTS COOKIE

COOKIE SHEET

COOKIE DOUGH

ROLLING PIN

FLATTEN FILLING

1¾"

LOW FAT
CHOCOLATE
WAFER

FAT FREE
FILLING

LOW FAT
CHOCOLATE
WAFER

1¾"

1¼"

3/16"

7/16"

⅛"

⅜"

SIDE

CRISPY

CREAMY

PROJECT: *NABISCO REDUCED-FAT OREO COOKIE*

NUTRITION STATS: *FAT-3.5G/CAL.-150* JOB NO. *N24756343-RFOC*

TOP SECRET RECIPES
VERSION OF

NABISCO SNACKWELL'S
APPLE RAISIN SNACK BARS

Nabisco unveiled a line of reduced-fat products in 1992 with the introduction of SnackWell's Devil's Food cookie cakes. The product was an instant hit with demand quickly outstripping the supply, leaving store shelves empty. The company poked fun at the situation with a series of humorous TV spots, showing the dweebish "Cookie Man" hounded by pushy shoppers trying to get their hands on his cookies. The successful product launch was followed up with the introduction of dozens of new SnackWell's products through the years, including Apple Raisin Snack Bars. Our clone uses a secret combination of unsweetened applesauce along with molasses and apple juice to keep the cake moist and tasty.

2 egg whites
1 cup plus 5 tablespoons
   granulated sugar
2 tablespoons brown sugar
1 tablespoon molasses
1 tablespoon dark corn syrup
½ cup unsweetened applesauce
¼ cup apple juice concentrate

3 tablespoons shortening
½ teaspoon vanilla
1½ cups all-purpose flour
¾ teaspoon salt
½ teaspoon cinnamon
¼ teaspoon baking soda
½ cup raisins

1. Preheat oven to 350 degrees.
2. In a large bowl, whip the egg whites with an electric mixer until they become thick. Do not use a plastic bowl for this.
3. Add the granulated sugar to the egg whites and continue to beat until the mixture forms soft peaks.

4. Add the brown sugar, molasses, dark corn syrup, applesauce, apple juice concentrate, shortening, and vanilla to the mixture while beating.
5. In a separate bowl, combine the remaining ingredients, except raisins.
6. While beating the wet mixture, slowly add the dry mixture.
7. Add the raisins, and combine by hand.
8. Lightly grease a 9 × 14-inch pan with a light coating of non-stick cooking spray. Be sure to coat the sides as well as the bottom of the pan. Dump about 3 tablespoons of sugar into the pan, then tilt and shake it so that a light layer of sugar coats the entire bottom of the pan and about halfway up the sides. Pour out the excess sugar.
9. Pour the batter into the pan and spread it evenly around the inside. Sprinkle a light coating of sugar—about 2 tablespoons—over the entire top surface of the batter. Gently shake the pan from side to side to evenly distribute the sugar over the batter. Bake for 25 to 28 minutes or until the cake begins to pull away from the sides of the pan.
10. Remove the cake from the oven and turn it out onto a cooling rack. When the cake has cooled, place it onto a sheet of wax paper on a cutting board and slice across the cake 6 times, creating 7 even slices. Next cut the cake lengthwise twice, into thirds, creating a total of 21 snack bars. When the bars have completely cooled, store them in a resealable plastic bag or an airtight container.

- MAKES 21 BARS.

Nutrition Facts

SERVING SIZE—1 BAR   TOTAL FAT (PER SERVING)—1.7 G
SERVINGS—21   CALORIES (PER SERVING)—120

• • • •

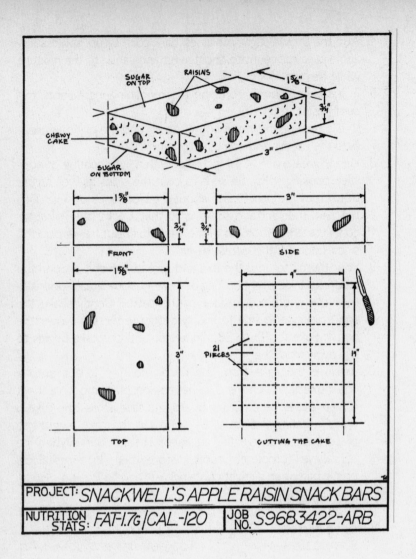

SUGAR ON TOP

RAISINS

1⅝"

¾"

CHEWY CAKE

3"

SUGAR ON BOTTOM

1⅝"

3/4"

¾"

FRONT

3"

SIDE

1⅝"

3"

TOP

9"

21 PIECES

14"

CUTTING THE CAKE

PROJECT: SNACKWELL'S APPLE RAISIN SNACK BARS

NUTRITION STATS: FAT-1.7g /CAL.-120

JOB NO. S9683422-ARB

TOP SECRET RECIPES VERSION OF

NABISCO SNACKWELL'S BANANA SNACK BARS

☆ ⚷ ⚫ ✎ ☯ ✂ ☞

In 1996, Nabisco built up its growing line of SnackWell's baked products with the introduction of low-fat snack bars in several varieties, including fudge brownie, golden cake, apple raisin (see previous recipe), and the chewy banana variety cloned here.

The secret to keeping the fat grams down in this recipe is the use of egg whites, molasses, and just a little shortening. But it's the banana puree that really slips in there to replace most of the fat while giving the cake real banana flavor and helping to keep it very moist.

2 egg whites
1 cup plus 5 tablespoons
   granulated sugar
2 tablespoons brown sugar
2 tablespoons molasses
1 ½ cups banana puree*
3 tablespoons shortening

¼ cup whole milk
½ teaspoon vanilla butter nut
   extract
1 ½ cups all-purpose flour
½ teaspoon salt
¼ teaspoon baking soda

1. Preheat oven to 350 degrees.
2. In a large bowl, whip the egg whites with an electric mixer until they become thick. Do not use a plastic bowl for this.
3. Add the sugar to the egg whites and continue to beat until the mixture forms soft peaks.
4. Add the brown sugar, molasses, banana puree, shortening,

*Puree whole bananas (approximately 3) in a food processor or blender until smooth and creamy.

milk, and vanilla butter nut flavoring to the mixture, beating after each addition.

5. In a separate bowl, combine the remaining ingredients.
6. While beating the wet mixture, slowly add the bowl of dry ingredients.
7. Lightly grease a 9 × 14-inch pan with a light coating of nonstick cooking spray. Be sure to coat the sides as well as the bottom of the pan. Dump about 3 tablespoons of sugar into the pan, then tilt and shake it so that a light layer of sugar coats the entire bottom of the pan and about halfway up the sides. Pour out the excess sugar.
8. Pour the batter into the pan and spread it evenly around the inside of the pan. Sprinkle a light coating of sugar—about 2 tablespoons—over the entire top surface of the batter. Gently shake the pan from side to side to evenly distribute the sugar over the batter. Bake for 25 to 28 minutes or until the cake begins to pull away from the sides of the pan.
9. Remove the cake from the oven and turn it out onto a cooling rack. When cake has cooled, place it onto a sheet of wax paper on a cutting board and slice across the cake 6 times, creating 7 even slices. Next cut the cake lengthwise twice, into thirds, creating a total of 21 snack bars. When the bars have completely cooled, store them in a resealable plastic bag or an airtight container.

- MAKES 21 BARS.

Nutrition Facts

SERVING SIZE—1 BAR	TOTAL FAT (PER SERVING)—1.8 G
SERVINGS—21	CALORIES (PER SERVING)—118

• • • •

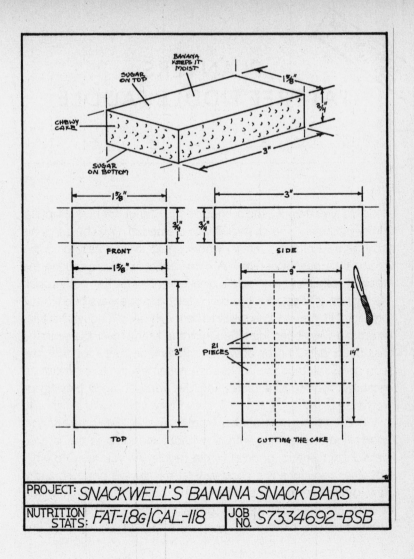

BANANA KEEPS IT MOIST

SUGAR ON TOP

CHEWY CAKE

SUGAR ON BOTTOM

1⅝"

3/4"

3"

FRONT

1⅝"

3/4"

SIDE

3"

3/4"

TOP

1⅝"

3"

CUTTING THE CAKE

9"

14"

21 PIECES

PROJECT: SNACKWELL'S BANANA SNACK BARS

NUTRITION STATS: FAT-1.8g/CAL.-118

JOB NO. S7334692-BSB

TOP SECRET RECIPES
VERSION OF

PLANTERS
FAT-FREE FIDDLE FADDLE

☆　　✄　　💣　　✒　　🎱　　✂　　☞

For many years now, the monocled Mr. Peanut has been Planters' nutty pitchman. The character was created in 1916 by a Virginia schoolboy, Anthony Gentile, who won $5 in a contest for drawing a "little peanut person." A commercial artist later added the top hat, cane, and monocle to make Mr. Peanut the stuffy socialite that he is today. But the character has not always been in the limelight. Planters' adman Bill McDonough says, "Though Mr. Peanut has always been identified with the brand, over the years he has been dialed up or down to different degrees." In 1999, the company dialed up the polite-and-proper legume to capitalize on nostalgia for the older folks and the young buyers' craving for retro chic.

Even though we think of Planters as the "nut company," you won't find a single nut, with or without monocle, in the fat-free version of Planters' popular Fiddle Faddle. All you need to whip together this clone is a good low-fat microwave popcorn and a few other common ingredients. This recipe requires your microwave to help coat the popcorn with a thin, crunchy coating of the tasty candy mixture.

1 teaspoon vegetable oil
½ cup light corn syrup
¾ cup light brown sugar
¼ cup water

½ teaspoon salt
¼ teaspoon vanilla extract
1 bag 94% fat-free microwave
　　popcorn

1. Combine the oil, corn syrup, brown sugar, water, and salt in a small saucepan over medium heat. Stir while bringing mixture

to a boil, then use a candy thermometer to bring mixture to 300 degrees (also known as the hard crack stage to candy makers).

2. When the candy reaches about 275 degrees, start cooking the popcorn by following the directions on the package. You want to time it so that the popcorn is done at approximately the same time as the candy. This way, the popcorn will be hot when you pour the candy over it.

3. When the candy has reached the right temperature, add the vanilla, then remove it from the heat. Pour the hot popcorn into a large plastic or glass bowl and quickly pour the candy over the top. Stir the popcorn so that the candy coats all of the pieces. To better help the candy coat the popcorn, place the bowl into the microwave and zap it for about 30 seconds on high. Stir the popcorn, and then, if necessary, microwave it for another 30 seconds. Stir it once more. By this time, the popcorn should be very well coated with a thin layer of the candy.

4. Quickly pour the popcorn out onto wax paper and spread it around to cool it.

5. When candy is cool, break it into bite-size pieces. Store it in a sealed container.

- MAKES 12 CUPS.

Nutrition Facts

SERVING SIZE—1 CUP   FAT (PER SERVING)—0 G
TOTAL SERVINGS—12   CALORIES (PER SERVING)—114

• • • •

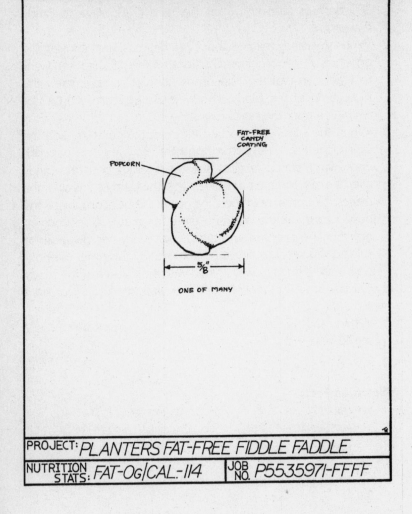

FAT-FREE
CANDY
COATING

POPCORN

5/8"

ONE OF MANY

PROJECT: *PLANTERS FAT-FREE FIDDLE FADDLE*	
NUTRITION STATS: *FAT-0g/CAL.-114*	JOB NO. *P5535971-FFFF*

TOP SECRET RECIPES
VERSION OF

RAINFOREST CAFE
REGGAE BEAT SEASONING

☆　　✌　　●❈　　✐　　◐　　✂　　☞

Walk inside Steve Schussler's house in Minneapolis, Minnesota, and you'd think you had stepped into a jungle. That's because seventeen years of research and seven years of construction went into re-creating a working rain forest inside the doors of his not-exactly-humble abode. This is how Steve presented the idea for his theme restaurant chain to the numerous potential investors. One of them, Lyle Berman, liked the idea and helped to provide the financing to open the first Rainforest Cafe in Minneapolis's Mall of America in 1994.

The popular chain has always used the Reggae Beat Seasoning in several of its recipes, including the Tropical Chicken Quartet (for which a conversion can be found on page 189). In 1998, Rainforest Cafe decided to bottle the spice and sell it in the gift shops attached to each of its thirty-three units around the world.

2 teaspoons minced dried onion	½ teaspoon cayenne pepper
1 teaspoon minced dried garlic	½ teaspoon ground black pepper
1 teaspoon granulated sugar	½ teaspoon allspice
¾ teaspoon salt	¼ teaspoon cinnamon
½ teaspoon crushed red pepper	¼ teaspoon ground clove
	dash cornstarch
	dash dried savory
	dash dried thyme

1. Combine all ingredients in a small cup or bowl.
2. Crush with the back of a spoon until finer in texture. Store in a covered container.

- MAKES ABOUT 3 TABLESPOONS.

• • • •

RAINFOREST CAFE
THE PLANT SANDWICH

☆   ✄   ●   ✎   ◉   ✂   ☞

Inside each Rainforest Cafe, customers are immersed in a thunder and lightning storm every twenty minutes. But don't worry, you don't have to bring your umbrella, since the rain only falls over specially designed troughs that recycle the water and ready it for the next downpour.

This sandwich was introduced in 1998 and uses Rainforest Cafe's delicious balsamic vinaigrette to marinate the mushrooms, making it one of the most delicious portobellos you've ever munched on. For this clone, prepare the vinaigrette and marinate the mushrooms a couple hours before you plan to assemble the sandwich.

BALSAMIC VINAIGRETTE

½ cup mayonnaise
5 teaspoons balsamic vinegar
1 tablespoon water
½ teaspoon cracked black pepper
¼ teaspoon garlic powder

⅛ teaspoon onion powder
⅛ teaspoon lemon juice
dash ground black pepper
dash salt

SANDWICH

4 portobello mushroom caps
1 medium zucchini, sliced thinly lengthwise
1 red bell pepper, seeded and quartered
4 large romaine lettuce leaves, chopped

2 tablespoons Caesar salad dressing
fat-free butter-flavored spray
a handful fresh spinach leaves
8 slices 7- or 9-grain bread

1. Prepare the balsamic vinaigrette by mixing the ingredients in a small bowl until smooth.
2. Place the mushroom caps into a large resealable plastic bag. Pour the balsamic vinaigrette into the bag, seal it up, and chill for an hour or two.
3. When the mushrooms have marinated, preheat your barbecue or indoor grill to high temperature.
4. Place the mushroom caps on the grill along with the zucchini and quartered bell pepper with the skin side down. Cook the zucchini for 3 to 4 minutes per side, and the mushrooms for 5 to 7 minutes per side. Leave the bell pepper with the skin side facing the heat for the entire time, until the skin is well charred.
5. In a medium bowl, toss the chopped lettuce with the Caesar dressing until well coated.
6. Preheat a large skillet over medium heat.
7. When you are ready to build the sandwiches, spray a light coating of butter spray over the face of each slice of bread. Grill the faces of the bread in the hot skillet until light brown.
8. Build each sandwich by first arranging a few spinach leaves on the face of one slice of bread, followed by about ¼ of the tossed romaine lettuce.
9. Place a grilled portobello mushroom cap on the lettuce.
10. Remove the charred skin from one of the bell pepper quarters and then slice the pepper in half, lengthwise. Place the two slices on the sandwich.
11. Cut one grilled zucchini slice in half, across the middle, and arrange the slices on the sandwich.
12. Top the sandwich with a grilled slice of bread. Cut the sandwich diagonally and stick a toothpick in each half. Repeat for the remaining sandwiches.

- MAKES 4 SANDWICHES.

Nutrition Facts

SERVING SIZE—1 SANDWICH   FAT (PER SERVING)—11 G
TOTAL SERVINGS—4   CALORIES (PER SERVING)—335

• • • •

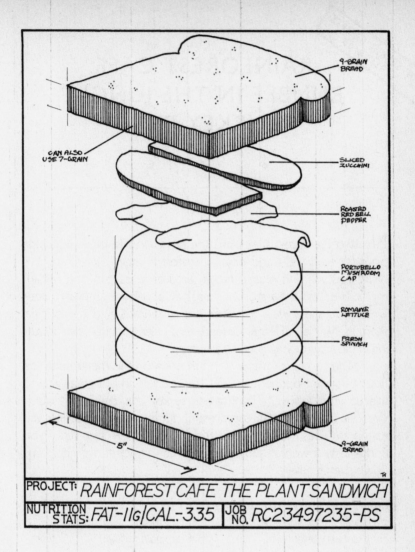

9-GRAIN BREAD

CAN ALSO USE 7-GRAIN

SLICED ZUCCHINI

ROASTED RED BELL PEPPER

PORTOBELLO MUSHROOM CAP

ROMAINE LETTUCE

FRESH SPINACH

5"

9-GRAIN BREAD

TW

PROJECT: *RAINFOREST CAFE THE PLANT SANDWICH*

NUTRITION STATS: *FAT-11g/CAL.-335* **JOB NO.** *RC23497235-PS*

TOP SECRET RECIPES
VERSION OF

RAINFOREST CAFE RUMBLE IN THE JUNGLE TURKEY PITA

☆　　✄　　✹　　✎　　◉　　✂　　☞

No two Rainforest Cafes are the same. While they all include plant-covered walls and ceilings, waterfalls, starry skies, and live birds, you will find many unique features in each of the restaurants. The Las Vegas store includes an aquarium archway under which you must walk to enter the restaurant, and the original store in the Mall of America features a talking banyan tree spouting ecological messages twice a minute.

The turkey pita sandwich has been on the menu since the first restaurant opened in 1994, and our clone is a great way to use up your leftover Thanksgiving turkey and cranberry sauce. We can use full-fat Caesar dressing for our clone, just like the restaurant uses, and still keep the fat reasonably low. But if you find a tasty lower-fat substitute, you can knock those fat grams down even further.

CRANBERRY RELISH (OPTIONAL)
1 16-ounce can whole berry
   cranberry relish
½ cup orange juice

¼ cup raisins
¼ cup gold raisins

PITA
10 large leaves romaine lettuce,
   chopped (5 to 6 cups)
¼ cup Caesar dressing
4 large pita breads

2 Roma tomatoes, sliced (16 slices)
1 cooked turkey breast, chilled
   (about 12 ounces)
½ cup French's french fried onions

1. Prepare the cranberry relish, if you plan to use it, by combining all of the ingredients in a medium saucepan over medium/high heat. Bring mixture to a boil, then reduce heat and simmer for 5 to 7 minutes. Remove mixture from heat, and cool. Pour mixture into a covered container and chill until cold.
2. Toss the lettuce with the Caesar dressing in a large bowl.
3. Wrap the pitas in a moist towel and heat in the microwave on high for about 1 minute or until all of the pitas are hot.
4. To make a sandwich, fold a pita like a taco and fill it with about ¼ the romaine lettuce.
5. Arrange four of the Roma tomato slices along one side of the pita.
6. Spoon 3 ounces (about ¾ cup) of the turkey over the lettuce and tomato slices, then sprinkle 2 tablespoons of fried onions on top. Serve with cranberry relish on the side, if desired. Repeat for the remaining sandwiches.

- MAKES 4 SANDWICHES.

Nutrition Facts

SERVING SIZE—1 SANDWICH	FAT (PER SERVING)—13 G
TOTAL SERVINGS—4	CALORIES (PER SERVING)—350

• • • •

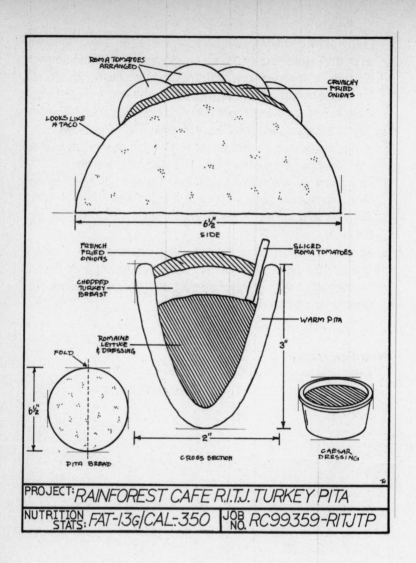

ROMA TOMATOES ARRANGED

CRUNCHY FRIED ONIONS

LOOKS LIKE A TACO

6½"
SIDE

FRENCH FRIED ONIONS

SLICED ROMA TOMATOES

CHOPPED TURKEY BREAST

WARM PITA

ROMAINE LETTUCE & DRESSING

3"

FOLD

6½"

2"

PITA BREAD

CROSS SECTION

CAESAR DRESSING

PROJECT: *RAINFOREST CAFE R.I.T.J. TURKEY PITA*

NUTRITION STATS: *FAT-13g/CAL.-350*

JOB NO. *RC99359-RITJTP*

TOP SECRET RECIPES
VERSION OF

SEVEN SEAS FREE
RED WINE VINEGAR
FAT-FREE DRESSING

☆   ✂   💣   ✎   ☯   ✂   ☞

The original version of this bright red dressing is made with a generous amount of oil and is filled with gobs of greasy fat grams. The trend toward fat-free foods was in its infancy when Seven Seas went to work on a nonfat variety of the Red Wine Vinegar Dressing that would taste as good as the original. They did a pretty darn good job, too. Just by tasting the Seven Seas version of this clone, it's hard to believe there's not a speck of fat in the bottle.

We can replace the oil by thickening the dressing with a top secret combination of water, cornstarch, and a little gelatin. A couple drops of food coloring will give your clone the bright, beet-red hue of the original. Of course, you can leave the coloring out of the recipe if you like, but when you see the color without the red, you'll understand why it's in there.

1 ⅓ cups water
¼ cup granulated sugar
2 teaspoons cornstarch
⅛ teaspoon Knox unflavored
   gelatin

1 ½ teaspoons dried minced
   onion
1 teaspoon salt
½ cup red wine vinegar
7 drops red food coloring

1. Combine water, sugar, cornstarch, gelatin, onion, and salt in a small saucepan. Whisk to dissolve cornstarch, then set pan over medium/low heat.
2. Heat mixture until boiling, stirring often. When mixture begins

to boil, cook for 2 additional minutes, stirring constantly, then remove from heat. Let mixture cool for 5 minutes.

3. Add vinegar and food coloring to saucepan and stir. Transfer dressing to a covered container and refrigerate—preferably overnight—before serving.

• MAKES 1½ CUPS.

Nutrition Facts

SERVING SIZE—2 TABLESPOONS   FAT (PER SERVING)—0 G
TOTAL SERVINGS—12   CALORIES (PER SERVING)—15

• • • •

TOP SECRET RECIPES VERSION OF

SEVEN SEAS FREE VIVA ITALIAN FAT-FREE DRESSING

☆   ✄   ●   ✎   ◉   ✂   ☞

Seven Seas dressings were first introduced by Anderson Clayton Foods back in 1964. Kraft Foods later picked up the brand, and Seven Seas today ranks number four in sales of salad dressings in the United States.

If it's a spice-filled Italian dressing you prefer, here's the secret technique to creating a clone of Seven Seas fat-free Italian dressing, using a combination of water, cornstarch, and gelatin.

1 1/3 cups water
1 1/2 tablespoons granulated sugar
2 teaspoons cornstarch
1 teaspoon salt
1/2 teaspoon dried minced onion
1/2 teaspoon dried minced garlic

1/2 teaspoon finely minced red bell pepper
1/2 teaspoon Italian seasoning
1/4 teaspoon gelatin
1/2 cup white vinegar
1 teaspoon dry nonfat buttermilk

1. Combine water, sugar, cornstarch, salt, onion, garlic, bell pepper, Italian seasoning, and gelatin in a small saucepan. Whisk to dissolve cornstarch, then set pan over medium/low heat.
2. Heat mixture until boiling, stirring often. When mixture begins to boil, cook for 1 additional minute, stirring constantly, then remove from heat.
3. Add vinegar and dry buttermilk to saucepan and stir. Transfer dressing to a covered container and refrigerate—preferably overnight—before serving.

• MAKES 1 1/2 CUPS.

TIDBITS

If you can't find dry buttermilk, you can substitute it with low-fat buttermilk—you know, the wet stuff. Measure 1 tablespoon into the dressing after you add the vinegar.

Nutrition Facts

SERVING SIZE—2 TABLESPOONS	FAT (PER SERVING)—0 G
TOTAL SERVINGS—12	CALORIES (PER SERVING)—10

• • • •

TOOTSIE ROLL
MIDGEES

☆   ⚘   ●   ✎   ◉   ✂   ☞

How would you react if your dentist suddenly whipped out a giant Tootsie Roll for you to bite down on so that he could make a mold of your teeth? Ask patients of a dentist in Philadelphia who does just that. This is just one of many facts that you learn researching the history of the Tootsie Roll, which, by the way, was named after the inventor's five-year-old daughter. Leo Hirschfield created the chewy brown candy in his small store in New York in 1896. In those days, the candy was hand rolled and delivered to customers by horse-drawn carriage. Over one hundred years later, more than forty-nine million Tootsie Rolls are produced each day from operations all over the world. And that's not counting the sixty bite-size clones—Tootsie Roll calls them "Midgees"—you'll make with this secret recipe.

1 cup granulated sugar
½ cup light corn syrup
2½ tablespoons shortening
4 teaspoons cocoa

2 tablespoons condensed skim milk
½ teaspoon vanilla

1. Combine sugar, corn syrup, shortening, and cocoa in a medium saucepan over medium/high heat.
2. Bring mixture to a boil, then reduce heat to medium, and simmer candy until temperature comes to 275 degrees on a candy thermometer.
3. Remove pan from heat. When bubbling stops, add condensed milk and beat in pan with electric mixer for about 30 seconds.

4. Add vanilla, then continue to beat candy until it begins to firm up and you can no longer beat it.
5. Pour candy out onto wax paper. When it is cool, divide candy into several portions and roll into long ropes that are approximately ½ inch thick.
6. Use a sharp knife to slice candy into 1⅛-inch-long portions.
7. Arrange the candy on a plate and let it sit out overnight so that it firms up.

• MAKES 60 PIECES.

Nutrition Facts

SERVING SIZE—6 PIECES   FAT (PER SERVING)—3 G
TOTAL SERVINGS—10   CALORIES (PER SERVING)—180

• • • •

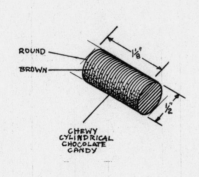

ROUND

BROWN

1⅛"

½"

CHEWY
CYLINDRICAL
CHOCOLATE
CANDY

PROJECT: *TOOTSIE ROLL MIDGEES*

NUTRITION
STATS: *FAT-3g/CAL.-180*

JOB
NO. *TR359074603-M*

LOW-FAT
TOP
SECRET
RECIPES
CONVERSIONS

TOP SECRET RECIPES
REDUCED-FAT VERSION OF

APPLEBEE'S
TEQUILA LIME CHICKEN

☆   ✄   💣   ✎   ●   ✂   ☞

This item has been a huge best-seller since it was first added to Applebee's menu in 1993 as promotional summer chow. The original version of this chicken dish is topped with an oil-based Mexi-ranch dressing, plus a melted cheddar and Monterey Jack cheese blend, making it every shade of tasty, yet brutal on the midriff. And customers freak over the marinade, which adds an addictive tang to the chicken breast that blends nicely with the other mellower ingredients. You'll need only a small amount of tequila to make this taste like the original—we're not making a margarita here! I learned the hard way that if you add more than the seemingly minuscule ¼ teaspoon of tequila to your chicken, it'll taste like it just got back from a bachelor party in Tijuana.

MARINADE

1 cup water
⅓ cup teriyaki sauce
2 tablespoons lime juice
2 teaspoons minced
    garlic

1 teaspoon mesquite liquid smoke
    flavoring
½ teaspoon salt
¼ teaspoon ground ginger
¼ teaspoon tequila

4 skinless chicken breast fillets

FAT-FREE MEXI-RANCH DRESSING

¼ cup fat-free mayonnaise
¼ cup fat-free sour cream
2 tablespoons reduced-fat milk
2 tablespoons water

2 teaspoons minced tomato
1 teaspoon minced canned
    jalapeño slices (nacho rings)
1 teaspoon minced onion

1 teaspoon white vinegar
1/4 teaspoon dried parsley
1/4 teaspoon salt
1/4 teaspoon Tabasco pepper
    sauce
1/8 teaspoon dried dillweed

1/8 teaspoon paprika
1/8 teaspoon cayenne pepper
1/8 teaspoon cumin
1/8 teaspoon chili powder
dash garlic powder
dash ground black pepper

1 cup reduced-fat shredded
    cheddar/Monterey Jack
    cheese blend

2 cups crumbled baked corn
    tortilla chips

1. Prepare the marinade by combining the ingredients in a medium bowl. Add the chicken to the bowl, cover, and chill for 2 to 3 hours.

2. Make the Mexi-ranch dressing by combining all of the ingredients in a medium bowl. Mix well until smooth, then cover the dressing and chill it until needed.

3. When you are ready to prepare the entrée, preheat the oven to high broil. Also preheat barbecue grill to high heat. When the barbie is hot, grill the marinated chicken breasts for 3 to 5 minutes per side, or until they're cooked all the way through.

4. Arrange the cooked chicken in a baking pan. Spread a layer of Mexi-ranch dressing over each piece of chicken followed by 1/4 cup of the shredded cheese blend. Broil the chicken for 1 to 2 minutes or just until the cheese melts.

5. Spread a bed of 1/2 cup of the crumbled tortilla chips on each of 4 plates. Slide a chicken breast onto the crumbled chips on each plate, and serve with your choice of rice and pico de gallo or salsa.

- SERVES 4 AS AN ENTRÉE.

Nutrition Facts (per serving)
SERVING SIZE—1 ENTRÉE   TOTAL SERVINGS—4

	LOW-FAT	ORIGINAL
CALORIES (APPROX.)	495	580
FAT (APPROX.)	15G	30G

• • • •

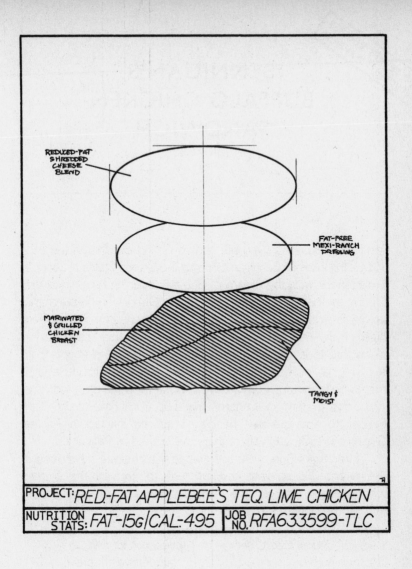

REDUCED-FAT
SHREDDED
CHEESE
BLEND

FAT-FREE
MEXI-RANCH
DRESSING

MARINATED
& GRILLED
CHICKEN
BREAST

TANGY &
MOIST

PROJECT: *RED-FAT APPLEBEE'S TEQ. LIME CHICKEN*

NUTRITION STATS: *FAT-15g/CAL-495*   JOB NO. *RFA633599-TLC*

TOP SECRET RECIPES
REDUCED-FAT VERSION OF

BENNIGAN'S
BUFFALO CHICKEN
SANDWICH

☆　　✌　　💣　　✏　　⚫　　✂　　☞

Visit the Bennigan's Web site and you'll find out that in the early 1900s, Irishman D. Bennigan came to the United States to work as a bartender with the dream of one day opening his own tavern. During the depression, Bennigan got his wish when he purchased an old, foreclosed bar, redecorated it, and opened the original Bennigan's Irish American Grill & Tavern. The "Our Story" page also explains that today all Bennigan's restaurants still use elements from that original location such as the brass rails, period pictures, and memorabilia hanging from the walls. What the Web page won't tell you is that this history is entirely made up. You'll have to dig a little deeper to find out that Bennigan's actually started in Atlanta, Georgia, in 1976, and was, at that time, owned by Pillsbury.

For this clone, we'll use a special technique developed in the secret underground test kitchens to prepare the chicken without frying. This will knock that fat down to just around one-third of the original.

1 skinless chicken breast fillet
½ cup all-purpose flour
½ teaspoon salt
½ cup egg substitute
   (or ½ cup milk)
nonstick cooking spray
2 tablespoons Louisiana hot sauce
   or Frank's Red Hot

1 tablespoon fat-free
   butter-flavored spread
1 hamburger bun
2 tomato slices
1 leaf green leaf lettuce
2 to 3 red onion rings
   (separated slices)

1. Wrap the chicken breast in plastic wrap and pound with a mallet until it is somewhere between ½ to ¼ inch thick and about the same size as the diameter of the bun.
2. Combine the flour and salt in a small bowl. Pour the egg substitute into another bowl. Drop the chicken breast into the bowl of flour and coat well. Coat the chicken with the egg substitute, and then put it back into the flour. When chicken is well coated, place it into the refrigerator to sit for 10 to 15 minutes. This is a good time to preheat the oven to 450 degrees.
3. Coat a baking pan with nonstick spray and place the chicken breast in it. Coat the top of the chicken breast with the cooking spray and bake it for 20 minutes or until it begins to brown.
4. Combine the hot sauce and fat-free spread in a plastic container big enough to hold the chicken. Be sure the container has a lid. When the chicken is done, place it into the plastic container with the spicy coating, cover, and gently shake the container until the chicken is well covered with the sauce.
5. Toast the face of the top and bottom bun and build the sandwich by turning the top bun over and arranging the lettuce on it. Stack the tomato slices, side by side, on the lettuce, then arrange 2 or 3 separated rings of onion on the sliced tomato.
6. Place the chicken breast on the face of the bottom bun, then turn the top half of the sandwich over onto the bottom. Serve immediately.

- MAKES 1 SANDWICH.

Nutrition Facts *(per serving)*
SERVING SIZE—1 SANDWICH   TOTAL SERVINGS—1

	LOW-FAT	ORIGINAL
CALORIES (APPROX.)	512	1038
FAT (APPROX.)	9G	27G

• • • •

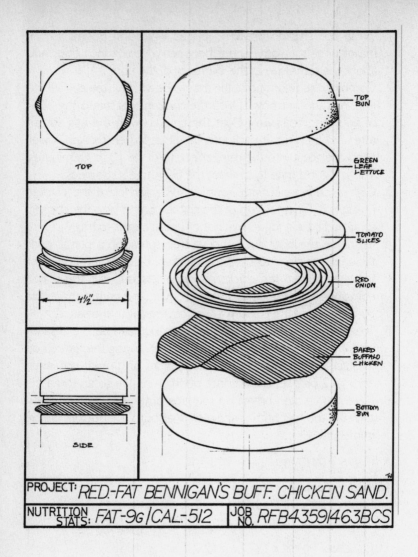

TOP

4½"

SIDE

TOP BUN

GREEN LEAF LETTUCE

TOMATO SLICES

RED ONION

BAKED BUFFALO CHICKEN

BOTTOM BUN

PROJECT: RED-FAT BENNIGAN'S BUFF. CHICKEN SAND.

NUTRITION STATS: FAT-9g / CAL.-512

JOB NO. RFB43591463BCS

TOP SECRET RECIPES
LOW-FAT VERSION OF

CALIFORNIA PIZZA KITCHEN SEDONA WHITE CORN TORTILLA SOUP

☆   ✄   ✦   ✎   ◉   ✂   ☞

When you get a steaming bowl of good tortilla soup plopped in front of you, it's tough to stop slurping until you hit bottom. California Pizza Kitchen has just such a soup, but the oil and fried tortilla chips put it a bit too far on the fat side. Never fear; we can make this delicious white corn tortilla soup taste just as good as the original without most of the oil and fat. Fat-free chicken broth stands in well for the regular stuff, and baked corn tortilla chips give the soup its traditional taste and texture. You'll want to use a hand blender for this one, if you've got one. If not, a regular blender or food processor will work fine to puree the soup so that it has the smooth consistency of the original but with only a minuscule two grams of fat per serving.

1 teaspoon olive oil
¼ cup minced white onion
2 cloves garlic, minced
3 cups frozen white corn, thawed
3 medium tomatoes, chopped
    (about 3 cups)
1 cup tomato sauce
2 tablespoons granulated sugar
1 teaspoon ground cumin

1 teaspoon salt
¼ teaspoon crushed red pepper
    flakes
⅛ teaspoon white pepper
½ teaspoon chili powder
2 14½-ounce cans fat-free
    chicken broth (4 cups)
1½ cups crumbled baked corn
    tortilla chips

OPTIONAL GARNISH

½ cup crumbled baked tortilla chips

½ cup fat-free shredded cheddar cheese

1 tablespoon minced cilantro

1. Preheat 1 teaspoon of oil in a large saucepan over medium heat.
2. Sauté the onion and garlic in the oil for a couple minutes or until the onions begin to turn translucent.
3. Add half of the corn and the remaining ingredients to the saucepan, then bring mixture to a boil. Reduce heat and simmer for 20 minutes.
4. Using an electric handheld blender, puree the soup until it is smooth. You may also puree the soup with a standard blender or food processor in batches.
5. Add the remaining corn to the soup, and simmer for an additional 20 minutes or until the soup is thick.
6. If desired, add some of the crumbled baked tortilla chips, cheddar cheese, and cilantro as a garnish and serve hot.

- SERVES 4.

Nutrition Facts (per serving)

SERVING SIZE—1½ CUPS   TOTAL SERVINGS—4

	LOW-FAT	ORIGINAL
CALORIES (APPROX.)	260	305
FAT (APPROX.)	2G	14G

• • • •

CARL'S JR.
RANCH CRISPY CHICKEN
SANDWICH

☆　　　✄　　　💣　　　✒　　　🎱　　　✂　　　☞

The 1980s were the beginning of tough times for one of the world's largest burger chains. Carl Karcher had built the little hot-dog cart he purchased for $311 in 1941 into a successful West Coast hamburger chain 600 units strong; but his luck was about to change. Carl took his company public, then opened several Carl's Jr. restaurants in Texas. The bottom line for the Texas stores fell way below expectations, and the stock began to skid. In 1988, Carl was charged with insider trading for selling stock just before its price fell, and he paid almost $1 million in fines. When poor Southern California real estate investments left him millions of dollars in debt, Carl was desperate to find a way out of the hole. He proposed to the board of directors that Carl's Jr. should sell Mexican food. The board rejected the plan, so Carl tried to fire its members. In 1993, the board voted to fire Carl instead, and the man with the vision was ousted from the very company he had founded.

For this reduced-fat clone of an excellent chicken sandwich, we'll make the ranch dressing from scratch with fat-free ingredients. Then we'll use a special Top Secret Recipes baking technique cooked up in the underground test kitchen that eliminates much of the fat we can't avoid when frying.

FAT-FREE RANCH DRESSING

1/3 cup fat-free mayonnaise

2 tablespoons fat-free sour cream

1 tablespoon reduced-fat
    buttermilk

1 1/2 teaspoons white vinegar

1 teaspoon granulated sugar

1/4 teaspoon lemon

1/8 teaspoon salt

1/8 teaspoon dried parsley

1/8 teaspoon onion powder

1/16 teaspoon dried dillweed

dash garlic

dash ground black pepper

1/2 teaspoon unflavored
    gelatin

2 teaspoons hot water

SANDWICH

1/4 cup egg substitute

1 cup water

1 cup flour

2 1/2 teaspoons salt

1 teaspoon paprika

1 teaspoon onion powder

1/8 teaspoon garlic powder

2 skinless chicken breast
    fillets

vegetable oil cooking spray

4 sesame seed hamburger
    buns

4 lettuce leaves

4 tomato slices

1. Prepare the ranch dressing by combining all ingredients except the gelatin and hot water in a medium bowl. Combine the gelatin with the hot water in a small bowl and stir to dissolve all of the gelatin. Add this to the other ingredients and stir well. Cover and chill (best to chill for at least a couple hours).

2. Preheat oven to 475 degrees.

3. Combine the egg substitute and water in a large, shallow bowl.

4. Combine the flour, salt, paprika, onion powder, and garlic powder in another shallow bowl.

5. Cut each chicken breast in half across the middle. Wrap each half in plastic wrap and pound it to about 1/4 inch thick. Trim each piece so that it is round.

6. Working with one fillet at a time, coat each with the flour, then dredge it in the egg and water mixture. Coat the chicken once again with the flour and set it aside until all of the fillets have been breaded.

7. Line a large baking sheet with aluminum foil. Spray the foil

with a generous coating of cooking oil. Place the chicken fillets on the baking sheet, then coat each one with a light layer of cooking spray.

8. Bake the fillets for 12 minutes, then crank the oven up to broil for 4 to 5 minutes, then flip the chicken over and broil for another 2 to 4 minutes or until the chicken is browned and crispy on both sides.

9. As chicken is cooking, prepare each sandwich by grilling the faces of the hamburger buns on a hot skillet over medium heat. Spread about 1½ teaspoons of the ranch dressing on the face of the top and bottom buns.

10. On the bottom bun, stack a leaf of lettuce and a tomato slice.

11. When the chicken is done cooking, stack a fillet over the tomato onto the bottom of the sandwich, then top off the sandwich with the top bun. Repeat for the remaining sandwiches.

- MAKES 4 SANDWICHES.

Nutrition Facts (per serving)

SERVING SIZE—1 SANDWICH   TOTAL SERVINGS—4

	LOW-FAT	ORIGINAL
CALORIES	580	620
FAT	11G	29G

• • • •

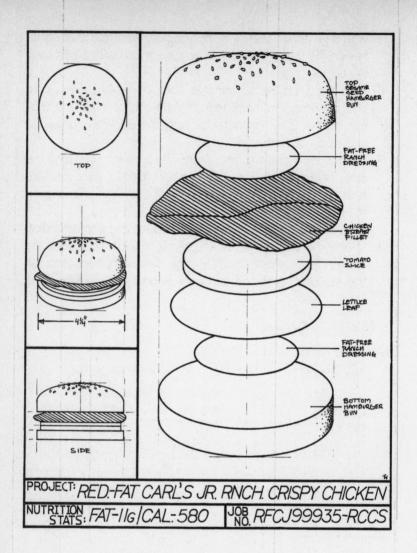

TOP

SIDE

4¼"

TOP
SESAME
SEED
HAMBURGER
BUN

FAT-FREE
RANCH
DRESSING

CHICKEN
BREAST
FILLET

TOMATO
SLICE

LETTUCE
LEAF

FAT-FREE
RANCH
DRESSING

BOTTOM
HAMBURGER
BUN

PROJECT: *RED.-FAT CARL'S JR. RNCH. CRISPY CHICKEN*

NUTRITION STATS: *FAT-11g / CAL.-580* JOB NO. *RFCJ99935-RCCS*

TOP SECRET RECIPES
REDUCED-FAT VERSION OF

CARL'S JR.
CHARBROILED CHICKEN
CLUB SANDWICH

Eight weeks after the board of directors locked seventy-six-year-old Carl Karcher out of his office in 1993, he was engineering a takeover of the "Happy Star" company that he had built over five decades. Crafty Carl found financier William P. Foley to assume his debts in exchange for stock and take control of the company as the new chairman of the board. Carl was named chairman emeritus and finally got his desk back. His plan to sell Mexican food at Carl's Jr. restaurants was later adopted and became a huge success for the chain, and almost all of the executives who had fired him have since left the company.

Here's one of Carl's delicious sandwiches that we can clone with much fewer fat grams by using turkey bacon, fat-free mayonnaise, and fat-free Swiss cheese. These substitutions for full-fat ingredients can bring the fat down from twenty-nine grams to just over ten without compromising that distinctive Carl's Jr. taste.

2 skinless chicken breast fillets
1/2 cup teriyaki marinade (thick style)
4 whole wheat hamburger buns
8 slices turkey bacon

1/4 cup fat-free mayonnaise
1 cup alfalfa sprouts
4 lettuce leaves
4 large tomato slices
4 slices fat-free Swiss cheese slices

1. Cut each chicken breast in half across the middle, then wrap the halves, one at a time, in plastic wrap. Pound each one with a mallet until it is about 1/4 inch thick.

2. Pour the teriyaki marinade over the meat. Cover and chill the meat and let it marinate for at least two hours. Marinating them overnight is even better.

3. When the chicken is well marinated, heat up a skillet and toast the face of each of the buns. Keep the pan hot. Preheat your barbecue or indoor grill to medium heat.

4. Fry the turkey bacon in the skillet for 5 to 6 minutes or until it's crispy, turning each slice over halfway through the cooking time.

5. As the bacon is frying, cook the chicken on the grill for 3 to 4 minutes per side or until done.

6. Build the sandwiches by first spreading ½ tablespoon of fat-free mayo on each toasted face of the buns.

7. Divide the sprouts into four even portions and stack a mound on each of the bottom buns.

8. On the sprouts, stack a lettuce leaf, and then a slice of tomato.

9. Place a piece of chicken on the tomato slice on each of the sandwiches.

10. Next, place a slice of Swiss cheese on the chicken, and then two pieces of bacon, crossed over each other.

11. Finish building the sandwiches by adding the top bun.

12. Microwave each sandwich for 15 seconds on high, and serve.

- MAKES 4 SANDWICHES.

Nutrition Facts (per serving)

SERVING SIZE—1 SANDWICH   TOTAL SERVINGS—4

	LOW-FAT	ORIGINAL
CALORIES	366	570
FAT	10.5G	29G

• • • •

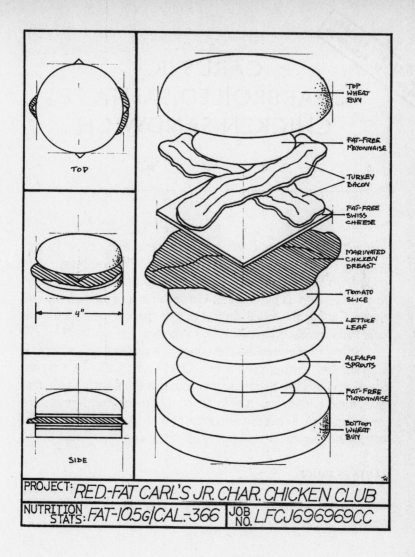

TOP

SIDE

4"

TOP WHEAT BUN

FAT-FREE MAYONNAISE

TURKEY BACON

FAT-FREE SWISS CHEESE

MARINATED CHICKEN DREAST

TOMATO SLICE

LETTUCE LEAF

ALFALFA SPROUTS

FAT-FREE MAYONNAISE

BOTTOM WHEAT BUN

PROJECT: *RED-FAT CARL'S JR. CHAR. CHICKEN CLUB*

NUTRITION STATS: *FAT-10.5g/CAL.-366*   **JOB NO.** *LFCJ696969CC*

TOP SECRET RECIPES
REDUCED-FAT VERSION OF

CARL'S JR.
CHARBROILED SANTA FE CHICKEN SANDWICH

In the last few years, Carl's Jr. has become one of the fastest-growing fast-food chains in the country. In 1997, the burger joint grew from 930 restaurants in nine states to nearly 3,900 in forty-four states with its purchase of Hardee's hamburger outlets. This makes Carl's Jr. the fourth-largest burger chain in the country, behind McDonald's, Burger King, and Wendy's.

One of the unique sandwiches that makes Carl's a popular stop for the lunch crowd is this Charbroiled Santa Fe Chicken Sandwich with the delicious spicy sauce. It's that tasty sauce that gives the real thing much of its fat, so by cloning it with nonfat ingredients, we can cut the grease on this sandwich to one-fifth of that of the original, while keeping all of the zing.

SANTA FE SAUCE

⅓ cup fat-free mayonnaise
¼ teaspoon paprika
¼ teaspoon curry powder

⅛ teaspoon cayenne pepper
⅛ teaspoon salt

SANDWICH

2 skinless chicken breast fillets
½ cup teriyaki marinade
   (thick style)
4 whole wheat hamburger buns

4 lettuce leaves
2 large canned mild green chili
   peppers, halved
4 slices fat-free American cheese

1. Make the sauce by combining all of the ingredients in a small bowl, and stir well. Cover and chill until needed.
2. Cut each chicken breast in half across the middle, and then wrap the halves, one at a time, in plastic wrap. Pound each one with a mallet until it is about ¼ inch thick.
3. Pour the teriyaki marinade over the chicken. Cover and chill the chicken and let it marinate for at least two hours. Marinating it overnight is even better.
4. When the chicken is well marinated, heat up a skillet and toast the face of each of the buns. You may also toast the buns in a toaster oven.
5. Cook the chicken on the grill for 3 to 4 minutes per side or until done.
6. Build the sandwiches by first spreading ½ tablespoon of the Santa Fe sauce on each toasted face of the buns.
7. Stack the lettuce on next.
8. Spread out a pepper half and place it on top of the lettuce on each sandwich. Depending on the size of the pepper, you may have to trim the pepper or add more. You want to have just enough to fit on the sandwich without too much excess falling over the side.
9. Place a piece of chicken on the pepper on each of the sandwiches.
10. Next, place a slice of American cheese on the chicken.
11. Finish building the sandwiches by adding the top bun.
12. Microwave each sandwich for 15 seconds on high.

• MAKES 4 SANDWICHES.

Nutrition Facts (per serving)

SERVING SIZE—1 SANDWICH   TOTAL SERVINGS—4

	LOW-FAT	ORIGINAL
CALORIES	305	530
FAT	5.5G	29G

• • • •

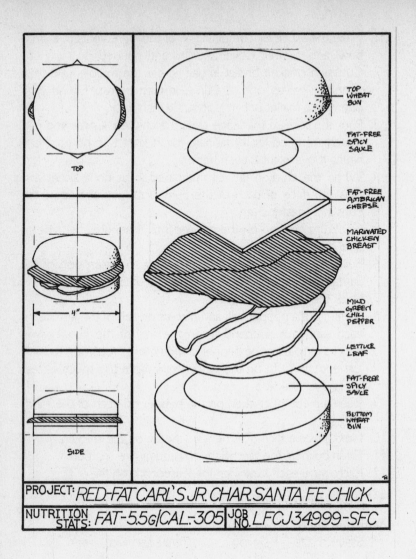

TOP

TOP
WHEAT
BUN

FAT-FREE
SPICY
SAUCE

FAT-FREE
AMERICAN
CHEESE

MARINATED
CHICKEN
BREAST

4"

MILD
GREEN
CHILI
PEPPER

LETTUCE
LEAF

FAT-FREE
SPICY
SAUCE

BOTTOM
WHEAT
BUN

SIDE

PROJECT: *RED.-FAT CARL'S JR. CHAR. SANTA FE CHICK.*

NUTRITION STATS: *FAT-5.5g/CAL.-305* JOB NO. *LFCJ34.999-SFC*

TOP SECRET RECIPES
REDUCED-FAT VERSION OF

CARL'S JR.
BACON SWISS CRISPY
CHICKEN SANDWICH

☆   ✄   ✎   ●   ✂   ☞

Helping Carl's Jr. rebound from its sales slump was a series of TV commercials featuring oversauced sandwiches that splattered ketchup and mayo onto floors, clothes, and shoes. The tag line, "If it doesn't get all over the place, it doesn't belong in your face," made sloppy synonymous with tasty.

If you look forward to messing up your clean clothes but don't need all the saturated fat that usually comes with this drippy fare, you'll want to give this clone a try. The fat-free ranch dressing saves you from oodles of nasty fat grams, and then the special baking technique that clones the taste and texture of deep frying eliminates a bunch more.

FAT-FREE RANCH DRESSING

1/3 cup fat-free mayonnaise
2 tablespoons fat-free sour cream
1 tablespoon reduced-fat
    buttermilk
1 1/2 teaspoons white vinegar
1 teaspoon granulated sugar
1/4 teaspoon lemon juice
1/8 teaspoon salt

1/8 teaspoon dried parsley
1/8 teaspoon onion powder
1/16 teaspoon dried dillweed
dash garlic
dash ground black pepper
2 teaspoons hot water
1/2 teaspoon unflavored
    gelatin

SANDWICH

8 slices lean turkey bacon, cooked
1/4 cup egg substitute

1 cup water
1 cup flour

123

2½ teaspoons salt
1 teaspoon paprika
1 teaspoon onion powder
⅛ teaspoon garlic powder
2 skinless chicken breast
   fillets

vegetable oil cooking spray
4 sesame seed hamburger buns
4 lettuce leaves
4 tomato slices
4 Kraft fat-free Swiss cheese
   singles

1. Prepare the ranch dressing by combining the ingredients in a small bowl. Cover and chill.
2. Preheat oven to 475 degrees.
3. Cook bacon following directions on package. Drain on paper towels and set aside.
4. Combine the egg substitute and water in a large, shallow bowl.
5. Combine the flour, salt, paprika, onion powder, and garlic powder in another shallow bowl.
6. Cut each chicken breast in half across the middle, and then wrap the halves, one at a time, in plastic wrap. Pound each one with a mallet until it is about ¼ inch thick. Trim each fillet until it is round.
7. Working with one fillet at a time, first coat each fillet with the flour, then dredge it in the egg and water mixture. Coat the chicken once again in the flour, and set it aside until all of the fillets have been breaded.
8. Line a large baking sheet with aluminum foil. Spray the foil with a generous coating of cooking oil. Place the chicken fillets on the baking sheet, then coat each one with a coating of cooking spray.
9. Bake the fillets for 12 minutes, then crank the oven up to broil for 4 to 5 minutes, then flip the chicken over and broil for another 2 to 4 minutes or until the chicken is browned and crispy on both sides.
10. As chicken is cooking, prepare each sandwich by grilling the face of the hamburger buns on a hot skillet over medium heat. Spread about 1½ teaspoons of the ranch dressing on the face of the top and bottom buns.
11. On the bottom bun, stack a leaf of lettuce and a tomato slice.
12. When the chicken is done cooking, place a fillet over the

tomato onto the bottom of the sandwich, then stack a slice of the fat-free Swiss cheese onto the chicken.

13. Arrange the bacon, crosswise, on top of the Swiss cheese, then top off the sandwich with the top bun. Repeat the stacking process for each of the remaining sandwiches.

• MAKES 4 SANDWICHES.

Nutrition Facts (per serving)

SERVING SIZE—1 SANDWICH   TOTAL SERVINGS—4

	LOW-FAT	ORIGINAL
CALORIES	660	720
FAT	19G	36G

• • • •

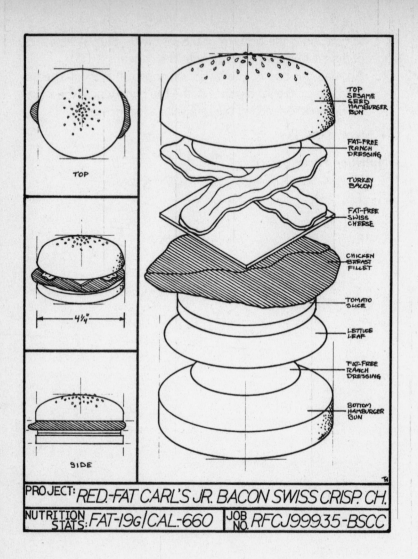

TOP

SIDE

4¼"

TOP SESAME SEED HAMBURGER BUN

FAT-FREE RANCH DRESSING

TURKEY BACON

FAT-FREE SWISS CHEESE

CHICKEN BREAST FILLET

TOMATO SLICE

LETTUCE LEAF

FAT-FREE RANCH DRESSING

BOTTOM HAMBURGER BUN

PROJECT: *RED.-FAT CARL'S JR. BACON SWISS CRISP. CH.*

NUTRITION STATS: *FAT-19G/CAL.-660*

JOB NO. *RFCJ99935-BSCC*

TOP SECRET RECIPES
FAT-FREE VERSION OF

CHEVYS
GARLIC MASHED POTATOES

☆   ⚷   💣   ✎   🎱   ✂   ☞

Everyone seems to love these delicious mashed potatoes at the "Fresh Mex" Mexican Food chain. Sure, mashed potatoes may seem like a healthy side dish, but when the traditional recipe includes cream and butter, it's easy to whip up quite a few fat grams in one small serving.

This recipe proves that mashed potatoes don't have to include fat to taste good. Use this recipe by itself or as part of the next tasty clone from this popular chain, Chevys Texas BBQ Wrap.

4 medium russet potatoes
1 tablespoon fat-free butter-
    flavored spread
1 tablespoon minced fresh garlic
    (3 to 4 cloves)

1¼ cups fat-free milk
¾ teaspoon salt
⅛ teaspoon ground black
    pepper

1. Preheat oven to 400 degrees.
2. Bake the potatoes by first spraying them with oil cooking spray and then baking them in the preheated oven for 1 hour or until they are tender. Cool.
3. Remove about half of the skin and mash the potatoes. Leave the rest of the skin in.
4. Melt the butter in a large saucepan over medium heat, then add the garlic and sauté for 5 minutes.
5. Add the potatoes and remaining ingredients to the pan and cook for 5 to 10 minutes while stirring often until mashed potatoes are very hot.

• SERVES 4.

Nutrition Facts *(per serving)*

Serving size—1 ¼ cups   Total servings—4

	Low-Fat	Original
Calories (approx.)	285	338
Fat (approx.)	0g	9g

• • • •

TOP SECRET RECIPES REDUCED-FAT VERSION OF

CHEVYS
TEXAS BBQ WRAP

☆   ✌   💣   🖊   🎱   ✂   ☞

Here's a great recipe that uses the previous Chevys clone recipe along with some cool new elements. In the restaurant, these are made with red chili tortillas. Since that sort of thing can be hard to find in the real world, especially in fat-free versions, we'll use plain flour fat-free tortillas. Except for the color, you can hardly tell the difference. You'll want to prepare several elements of this recipe ahead of time. The relish and slaw is best when made the day before, and the chicken will have to marinate for an hour or so before you grill it. Be sure to prepare the garlic mashed potatoes well ahead of time, following the instructions on page 127. And be real hungry.

CORN AND PEPPER RELISH

uncooked corn cut from 1 ear of
    corn (about 1/2 cup)
2 tablespoons diced red bell pepper
2 tablespoons diced green bell
    pepper

2 tablespoons diced Spanish
    onion
pinch minced fresh cilantro
dash salt

DRESSING

1 tablespoon white vinegar
1 tablespoon water
1/2 teaspoon granulated sugar

1/8 teaspoon cayenne pepper
1/8 teaspoon plus a pinch cumin
1 teaspoon light mayonnaise

CHIPOTLE SLAW

1 1/4 cups shredded red cabbage

1/4 cup green cabbage

MESQUITE MARINADE

1 cup water	1 teaspoon salt
2 teaspoons mesquite-flavored liquid smoke	dash ground black pepper

2 skinless chicken breast fillets

BEANS

1 15-ounce can black beans, with liquid	⅛ teaspoon salt
¼ teaspoon chili powder	dash garlic powder

4 large fat-free flour tortillas	½ cup spicy BBQ sauce
4 cups garlic mashed potatoes (from page 127)	(from page 133)

1. Prepare the corn and pepper relish by combining the ingredients in a medium bowl.
2. Prepare the dressing for the relish and chipotle slaw by mixing the vinegar, water, sugar, cayenne pepper, and cumin in a small bowl. Stir to dissolve the sugar. Measure 1 tablespoon of this mixture and add it to the corn and pepper relish. Cover the relish and chill it until needed. This relish is best when made the day before.
3. Add a teaspoon of light mayonnaise and an additional pinch of cumin to the small bowl of dressing. Whisk the mixture to help the mayonnaise blend in. Add this remaining dressing to the shredded cabbage in a medium bowl. Stir well, then cover and chill until needed. This slaw is also best when chilled overnight.
4. One hour before you are ready to make the dish, prepare the mesquite marinade by mixing the ingredients in a medium bowl. Add the chicken breast fillets to the marinade, cover, and chill for 1 hour.
5. If you haven't already done so, prepare the garlic mashed potatoes from page 127 and the spicy BBQ sauce from page 133.

6. When chicken has marinated, preheat grill on high temperature.
7. Prepare the black beans by combining the beans (with liquid), chili powder, salt, and garlic powder in a small saucepan over low heat. Simmer for 15 to 20 minutes or until beans boil and mixture becomes thicker.
8. Spray each side of the chicken with a light coating of nonstick oil cooking spray. Lightly salt and pepper each side of each chicken breast and grill for 4 to 5 minutes per side or until done. After removing the chicken from the grill, chop it into bite-size pieces. Remove about ⅓ of the spicy barbecue sauce and mix it in with the diced chicken in a medium bowl.
9. Wrap the tortillas in moist paper towels (or place them in a tortilla steamer) and microwave on high temperature for 30 to 45 seconds or until tortillas are hot and pliable.
10. Build each wrap by first spooning about ½ cup of the garlic mashed potatoes into the center of a hot tortilla. Spoon ¼ of the black beans onto the potatoes, followed by ¼ of the chicken. Spread ¼ of the slaw onto the chicken and then ¼ of the corn and pepper relish. Fold in the ends of the tortilla and then roll it up from the bottom into a tight package. Drizzle some of the leftover spicy BBQ sauce over the top of the wrap, slice it through the middle, and serve. Repeat for the remaining ingredients.

• SERVES 4 AS AN ENTRÉE.

Nutrition Facts (per serving)

SERVING SIZE—1 WRAP   TOTAL SERVINGS—4

	LOW-FAT	ORIGINAL
CALORIES (APPROX.)	515	644
FAT (APPROX.)	5G	15G

• • • •

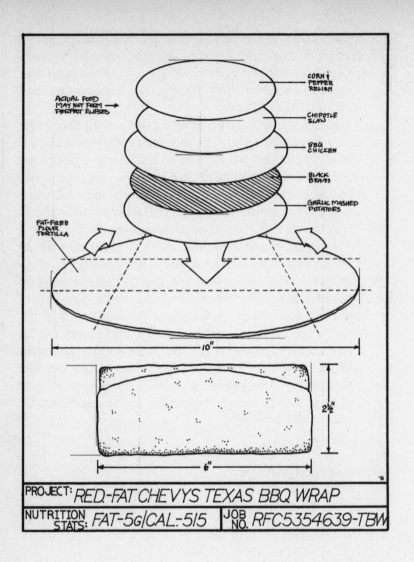

ACTUAL FOOD
MAY NOT FORM →
PERFECT ELIPSES

CORN &
PEPPER
RELISH

CHIPOTLE
SLAW

BBQ
CHICKEN

BLACK
BEANS

GARLIC MASHED
POTATOES

FAT-FREE
FLOUR
TORTILLA

10"

2½"

6"

PROJECT: *RED.-FAT CHEVYS TEXAS BBQ WRAP*

NUTRITION STATS: *FAT-5g/CAL.-515*

JOB NO. *RFC5354639-TBW*

CHEVYS MESQUITE-GRILLED BBQ CHICKEN QUESADILLA

☆   ✌   💣   ✏   ☯   ✂   ☞

With this secret recipe it isn't necessary to cook the chicken over a mesquite grill as they do in the restaurant chain. Sure, you could get some mesquite wood chips and throw 'em on your barbecue or you can use that charcoal that has mesquite in it. But an easier way to get the flavor of mesquite—especially if all you've got is a gas grill—is to soak the chicken in a marinade made with mesquite-flavored liquid smoke. Again, in the restaurant these quesadillas are made with red chili tortillas. Since these can be a drag to track down, especially in fat-free versions, we will use plain fat-free flour tortillas.

MESQUITE MARINADE

½ cup water
1 teaspoon mesquite-flavored liquid smoke

½ teaspoon salt
dash ground black pepper

1 skinless chicken breast fillet

SPICY BBQ SAUCE

½ cup Bull's-Eye Original BBQ sauce

¼ teaspoon cayenne pepper
dash chili powder

⅓ cup sliced red bell pepper
⅓ cup sliced green bell pepper
⅓ cup sliced Spanish onion

2 large (12-inch) fat-free flour tortillas
1⅓ cups shredded Monterey Jack cheese

1. Prepare the marinade by combining the ingredients in a medium bowl. Add chicken breast fillet to the bowl, cover, and chill for one hour.
2. When the chicken is finished marinating, preheat your grill to high temperature.
3. As grill is heating, prepare the spicy BBQ sauce by mixing the ingredients in a small bowl.
4. Throw the chicken on the grill and cook it for 4 to 5 minutes per side or until it's done. When the chicken is done cooking, chop it into bite-size pieces.
5. Spray a light coating of nonstick cooking spray on a medium skillet over medium heat. Sauté the sliced peppers and onion in the pan for 4 or 5 minutes or until the veggies start to brown.
6. Set a large skillet over medium/low heat.
7. Put one flour tortilla in the skillet and sprinkle ⅓ cup of cheese over half of the tortilla. Spoon half of the vegetables over the cheese, followed by half of the chicken.
8. Spoon a generous portion of the spicy BBQ sauce over the chicken, followed by another ⅓ cup of cheese.
9. Fold the other side of the tortilla over the filling, and press down so that it stays in place.
10. By this time, the cheese on the bottom should be melted. If not, wait another minute or so, then flip the quesadilla over and heat for another couple minutes or until all of the cheese has melted.
11. Slide the quesadilla onto a plate and slice it into 4 pieces. Repeat for the second quesadilla and serve immediately with salsa from page 28.

- SERVES 4 AS AN APPETIZER.

Nutrition Facts *(per serving)*
SERVING SIZE—2 PIECES   TOTAL SERVINGS—4

	LOW-FAT	ORIGINAL
CALORIES (APPROX.)	278	400
FAT (APPROX.)	10G	20G

• • • •

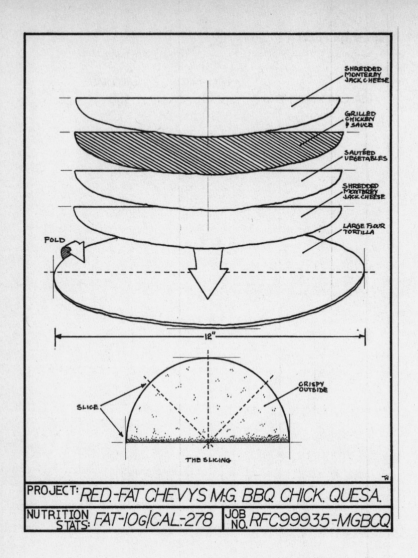

SHREDDED MONTEREY JACK CHEESE

GRILLED CHICKEN & SAUCE

SAUTÉED VEGETABLES

SHREDDED MONTEREY JACK CHEESE

LARGE FLOUR TORTILLA

FOLD

12"

SLICE

CRISPY OUTSIDE

THE SLICING

PROJECT: RED.-FAT CHEVYS M.G. BBQ CHICK. QUESA.

NUTRITION STATS: FAT-10G/CAL.-278

JOB NO. RFC99935-MGBCQ

TOP SECRET RECIPES
REDUCED-FAT VERSION OF

CHILI'S
BONELESS BUFFALO WINGS

☆　　⚓　　💣　　✒　　◉　　✂　　☞

Not only does this conversion for Chili's new appetizer give us the zesty flavor of traditional Buffalo chicken wings without the bones or fatty skin, but I've come up with a way to bake the chicken, rather than fry it, so that we eliminate even more of those pesky fat grams. These "wings" are actually nuggets sliced from chicken breast fillets that have been breaded and fried and smothered with the same type of spicy wing sauce used on typical wings, but without the butter. If you like Buffalo wings, you'll love this reduced-fat clone, which can be served up with some celery sticks and fat-free bleu cheese dressing on the side for dipping. Party down.

1 cup all-purpose flour
2 teaspoons salt
¼ teaspoon ground black pepper
¼ teaspoon cayenne pepper
¼ teaspoon paprika
¼ cup egg substitute
1 cup reduced-fat (2%) milk

2 skinless chicken breast fillets
oil cooking spray
¼ cup Frank's or Crystal Louisiana
　　hot sauce
2 tablespoons fat-free butter-
　　flavored spread
2 tablespoons water

ON THE SIDE
Fat-free bleu cheese dressing
　　(for dipping)

celery sticks

1. Preheat oven to 475 degrees.
2. Combine flour, salt, peppers, and paprika in a medium bowl.
3. Whisk egg and milk together in a small bowl.

4. Slice each chicken breast into 5 or 6 pieces.
5. Working with one or two pieces of chicken at a time, dip each piece into the egg mixture, then into the breading blend; then repeat the process so that each piece of chicken is double-coated.
6. Coat a baking sheet with a generous portion of the oil cooking spray. Arrange the chicken on the baking sheet and then spray a light coating over the top of each piece.
7. Bake the chicken for 10 to 12 minutes or until it begins to brown. Crank the heat up to broil, and continue to cook the chicken for 2 to 4 more minutes or until the surface begins to become golden brown and crispy.
8. As the chicken cooks, combine the hot sauce, butter-flavored spread, and water in a small saucepan over medium/low heat. Cook just until the mixture begins to bubble, then remove the sauce from the heat and cover it until it's needed.
9. When the chicken pieces are cooked, remove them from the oven and let them cool for a couple minutes. Place the chicken into a covered container such as Tupperware or a large jar with a lid. Pour the sauce over the chicken in the container, cover, and then shake gently until each piece of chicken is coated with sauce. Pour the chicken onto a plate and serve the dish with fat-free bleu cheese dressing and sliced celery sticks on the side.

• SERVES 4 AS AN APPETIZER.

Nutrition Facts *(per serving)*

SERVING SIZE—3 PIECES   TOTAL SERVINGS—4

	LOW-FAT	ORIGINAL
CALORIES (APPROX.)	200	280
FAT (APPROX.)	5.5G	15G

• • • •

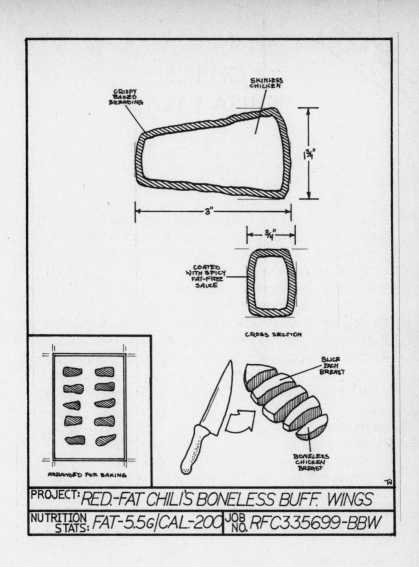

CRISPY BAKED BREADING

SKINLESS CHICKEN

1 3/4"

3"

3/4"

COATED WITH SPICY FAT-FREE SAUCE

CROSS SECTION

ARRANGED FOR BAKING

SLICE EACH BREAST

BONELESS CHICKEN BREAST

TW

PROJECT: RED.-FAT CHILI'S BONELESS BUFF. WINGS

NUTRITION STATS: FAT-5.5g/CAL.-200

JOB NO. RFC335699-BBW

TOP SECRET RECIPES
REDUCED-FAT VERSION OF

CHILI'S
FAJITA SALAD

☆   ✄   💣   ✎   ◉   ✂   ☞

This big salad of mixed greens, fajita steak, pico de gallo, black beans, bell peppers, corn and guacamole comes slathered with two types of salad dressings plus fried tortilla chips, making the restaurant version a fat-filled fiesta.

When made from scratch with this secret Top Secret Recipes formula, the two dressings are made fat-free, knocking the fat grams down to around a third of what you munch down in the original. There are several components here in this conversion, but this recipe makes four of the huge entrée-size salads, and the results are worth the effort. This recipe clones the steak version of the salad, but you can also replace the beef with chicken.

MARINADE

⅔ cup water
1 tablespoon vegetable oil
2 tablespoons soy sauce
1 large clove garlic, pressed
1 tablespoon granulated sugar
1 teaspoon liquid smoke

1 teaspoon chili powder
½ teaspoon salt
½ teaspoon cayenne pepper
½ teaspoon ground black
   pepper
½ teaspoon onion powder

4 sirloin steaks (approximately
   4 ounces each)

FAT-FREE CHIPOTLE RANCH DRESSING

¼ cup fat-free mayonnaise
¼ cup fat-free sour cream
3 tablespoons buttermilk

1 tablespoon water
1½ teaspoons white vinegar
¼ teaspoon plus ⅛ teaspoon salt

⅛ teaspoon dried parsley
⅛ teaspoon onion powder
dash dried dillweed

dash garlic powder
dash ground black pepper

FAT-FREE SANTA FE DRESSING
⅓ cup fat-free Catalina dressing
1 tablespoon stone ground
   mustard
1 tablespoon water
½ teaspoon lemon juice

½ teaspoon white vinegar
¼ teaspoon cumin
¼ teaspoon cayenne pepper
⅛ teaspoon ground black pepper
⅛ teaspoon dried thyme

PICO DE GALLO
2 medium tomatoes, chopped
½ cup chopped Spanish onion
1 jalapeño, seeded and diced
   (about 2 tablespoons)

2 teaspoons finely chopped
   cilantro
⅛ teaspoon salt

SOUTHWESTERN GARNISH
1 cup frozen corn, thawed
⅔ cup canned black beans,
   drained and rinsed

¼ cup diced red bell pepper
¼ cup diced green bell pepper
⅛ teaspoon salt

MIXED GREENS
1 head iceberg lettuce, chopped
1 head romaine lettuce, chopped

1 carrot, shredded
1 cup shredded red cabbage

2 cups crumbled baked corn
   tortilla chips

1 cup guacamole

1. Prepare the marinade by combining all of the ingredients in a small bowl. Stir well. Add meat to marinade, cover, and chill for at least 4 hours. Marinating overnight is even better.
2. While meat marinates, prepare the dressings and garnishes. Combine the ingredients for each of the dressings in separate small bowls. Stir well, then cover and chill. Hope you have some more small, clean bowls, because you're going to need a few more for the garnishes. Combine the ingredients for

each of the garnishes in separate bowls, then cover and chill these as well.

3. If you have some more room in the fridge, you may want to prepare your greens now by combining the lettuces with the carrot and cabbage in a large salad bowl. Cover this bowl and chill it until you are ready to assemble the salads. You may choose to save this step until you are ready to grill the meat.

4. When the meat has marinated, preheat your barbecue grill to high heat.

5. Grill the steaks for 5 to 7 minutes per side or until done.

6. While the meat is grilling, prepare the salad by tossing the mixed greens with the Santa Fe dressing in a large bowl.

7. Spoon approximately ⅛ of the greens onto each of four plates.

8. Sprinkle ¼ of the pico de gallo onto the greens on each plate, followed by ¼ of the Southwestern garnish.

9. Spoon ¼ of the remaining greens onto the salad on each plate.

10. Sprinkle ¼ of the tortilla chips over the greens on each plate.

11. Drizzle the ranch dressing over the salads with a sweeping motion. If you have an empty squirt bottle, such as an empty mustard or honey bottle, fill that with the dressing and use it to drizzle the dressing across the salad.

12. When the meat is done grilling, slice each steak into bite-size strips and arrange it over the top of each salad.

13. Spoon the guacamole onto the top of each of the sliced steaks and serve.

- SERVES 4 AS AN ENTRÉE.

Nutrition Facts (per serving)
SERVING SIZE—1 SALAD   TOTAL SERVINGS—4

	LOW-FAT	ORIGINAL
CALORIES (APPROX.)	591	784
FAT (APPROX.)	15G	45G

• • • •

TOP SECRET RECIPES
REDUCED-FAT VERSION OF

CHILI'S
MARGARITA GRILLED TUNA

☆   ✌   ✺   ✐   ☯   ✂   ☞

A plateful of rice and black beans are topped with a corn tortilla, garlic aioli, lettuce, pico de gallo and a fresh tuna steak smothered with chipotle ranch dressing.

There are many opportunities to obliterate fat in this one, most easily in the garlic aioli and chipotle ranch dressing. The tuna you purchase may come in thick eight-ounce steaks. If so, slice the tuna through the center, making two thinner four-ounce pieces. With the rice, black beans, and toppings, this dish is an entire meal on its own. And, oh my, what an impressive presentation.

GARLIC AIOLI

1 head garlic
1 teaspoon olive oil
2 tablespoons fat-free mayonnaise

½ teaspoon lemon juice
¼ teaspoon vinegar
dash salt

FAT-FREE SANTA FE DRESSING

⅓ cup fat-free Catalina dressing
1 tablespoon stone ground
   mustard
1 tablespoon water
½ teaspoon lemon juice

½ teaspoon white vinegar
¼ teaspoon cumin
¼ teaspoon cayenne pepper
⅛ teaspoon ground black pepper
⅛ teaspoon dried thyme

PICO DE GALLO

2 medium tomatoes, chopped
½ cup chopped Spanish onion
1 jalapeño, seeded and diced
   (about 2 tablespoons)

2 teaspoons finely chopped
   cilantro
⅛ teaspoon salt

MARGARITA MARINADE

1 cup sweet and sour mix
2 teaspoons tequila

1 teaspoon lime juice

SEARING SPICE

1/4 cup olive oil
2 tablespoons chopped onion
2 cloves garlic
1 teaspoon cayenne pepper
1 1/2 teaspoons Schilling poultry
   seasoning

1 1/2 teaspoons salt
1/2 teaspoon paprika
1/2 teaspoon lemon juice
1/4 teaspoon ground black
   pepper

RICE

2 1/3 cups chicken stock
1 tablespoon butter
1 cup converted or long-
   grain white rice (not
   instant rice)
1/4 cup frozen corn
2 tablespoons diced carrots

2 tablespoons diced red bell
   pepper
2 tablespoons diced celery
1 tablespoon diced white onion
1/2 teaspoon salt
1/2 teaspoon dried parsley
dash ground black pepper

BLACK BEANS

1 teaspoon olive oil
1/3 cup diced white onion
1/4 cup diced red bell pepper

2 15-ounce cans black beans with
   liquid

4 4-ounce tuna fillets (2 8-ounce
   fillets cut through the center)

4 corn tostada shells
1 1/3 cups shredded iceberg lettuce

1. Preheat the oven to 325 degrees.
2. Prepare the garlic aioli by roasting the garlic: Cut 1/2 inch off
   the top of the papery skin from the garlic, but leave enough
   so that the cloves stay together. Place the head of garlic in a
   small casserole dish or baking pan, drizzle the olive oil over it,
   and cover it with a lid or foil. Bake for 1 hour. Remove the
   garlic and let it cool until you can handle it.
3. Prepare the dressing, pico de gallo, and margarita marinade

by combining the ingredients in small bowls. Cover and chill these mixtures until later.

4. Pour the searing spice ingredients into a blender or food processor and puree until you have a smooth mixture with the consistency of pesto. Set this aside.

5. Prepare the rice by bringing chicken stock and butter to a boil over medium/high heat. Add the remaining ingredients to the pan, stir, and cover. Reduce heat to low and simmer for 20 to 25 minutes or until liquid has been absorbed and the rice is cooked.

6. Prepare black beans by pouring a teaspoon of olive oil into a saucepan. Use a paper towel to wipe the oil around the pan and then set it over medium heat. Sauté the diced onion and red bell pepper in the oil for a minute or two and then add the cans of black beans, along with the liquid, to the pan. Reduce heat to medium/low, and simmer until needed. Stir occasionally.

7. Preheat a large skillet over medium heat.

8. Place your tuna fillets into the margarita marinade. Marinate for only 15 minutes and then dry the tuna on paper towels. Be sure not to marinate the tuna for more than 15 minutes or the lime juice will begin to toughen the fish.

9. Place the four tostada shells into an oven preheated to 350 degrees. Turn off the heat after 5 minutes and let the shells sit in the oven until they are needed.

10. Brush the top of each of the fillets with the searing spice blend and turn them with the spice side down onto the hot skillet. Brush additional searing spice over the top of each fillet. Cook the fish for about 2 minutes per side or until the fish is browned on both sides and cooked through.

11. Build each dish by spooning about ¾ cup of rice into the center of a dinner plate. Encircle the rice with a portion of the black beans. Spread a thin layer of garlic aioli onto a tostada shell and place it on the rice. Sprinkle about ⅓ cup of lettuce onto the shell next. Place a tuna fillet on top of the lettuce. Drizzle the Santa Fe dressing over the entire dish with a sweeping motion. Finally, pile about ⅓ cup of the pico

de gallo on top of the tuna. Repeat for the remaining plates and serve immediately.

- SERVES 4 AS AN ENTRÉE.

Nutrition Facts *(per serving)*

SERVING SIZE—1 ENTRÉE   TOTAL SERVINGS—4

	LOW-FAT	ORIGINAL
CALORIES (APPROX.)	691	899
FAT (APPROX.)	16G	38G

• • • •

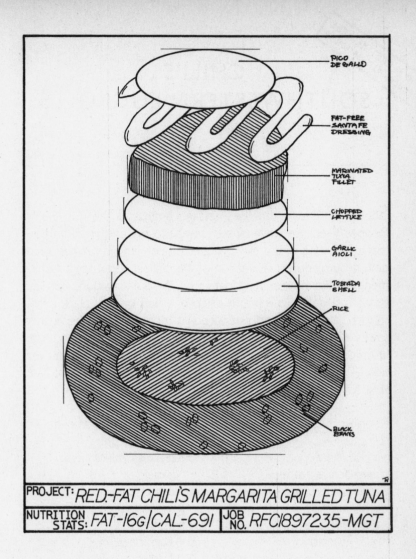

PICO
DE GALLO

FAT-FREE
SANTA FE
DRESSING

MARINATED
TUNA
FILLET

CHOPPED
LETTUCE

GARLIC
AIOLI

TOSTADA
SHELL

RICE

BLACK
BEANS

PROJECT: *RED.-FAT CHILI'S MARGARITA GRILLED TUNA*

NUTRITION STATS: *FAT-16g/CAL.-691* | **JOB NO.** *RFC1897235-MGT*

TOP SECRET RECIPES
REDUCED-FAT VERSION OF

CHILI'S
SOUTHWESTERN EGGROLLS

☆   ✂   💣   ✏   ◉   ✂   ☞

Spend some time on the message boards at the Top Secret Recipes Web site (*www.topsecretrecipes.com*), and you'll find out that this is one of the most requested conversion recipes. Here now is our reduced-fat version of the tastiest appetizer on Chili's menu. Unlike the real thing that's fried, this amazing clone is baked. Inside is a delicious mixture of corn, green onions, black beans, spinach, jalapeño peppers, reduced-fat Monterey Jack cheese, and spices. Once these babies come out of the oven hot and crispy, just slice 'em in half and serve 'em surrounding a killer low-fat version of the tasty avocado ranch dressing. It's a taste bud party, and your tongue's invited!

1 skinless chicken breast fillet
salt
ground black pepper
1 teaspoon vegetable oil
2 tablespoons minced red bell pepper
2 tablespoons minced green onion
1/3 cup frozen corn
1/4 cup canned black beans, rinsed and drained
2 tablespoons frozen spinach, thawed and drained

2 tablespoons diced, canned jalapeño peppers
1/2 tablespoon minced fresh parsley
1/2 teaspoon cumin
1/2 teaspoon chili powder
1/4 teaspoon salt
dash cayenne pepper
3/4 cup shredded reduced-fat (2%) Monterey Jack cheese
5 7-inch flour tortillas

LOW-FAT AVOCADO-RANCH DIPPING SAUCE

¼ cup smashed, fresh avocado
   (about ½ avocado)
¼ cup fat-free mayonnaise
¼ cup fat-free sour cream
1 tablespoon buttermilk
1 ½ teaspoons white vinegar

⅛ teaspoon salt
⅛ teaspoon dried parsley
⅛ teaspoon onion powder
dash dried dillweed
dash garlic powder
dash ground black pepper

oil cooking spray

GARNISH

2 tablespoons chopped tomato   1 tablespoon chopped onion

1. Preheat barbecue grill to high heat.
2. Rub the chicken breast with some vegetable oil, then grill it on the barbecue for 4 to 5 minutes per side or until done. Lightly salt and pepper each side of the chicken while it cooks. Set chicken aside until it cools down enough to handle.
3. Preheat 1 teaspoon of vegetable oil in a medium-size skillet over medium/high heat.
4. Add the red pepper and green onion to the pan and sauté for a couple minutes until tender.
5. Dice the cooked chicken into small cubes and add it to the pan. Add the corn, black beans, spinach, jalapeño peppers, parsley, cumin, chili powder, salt, and cayenne pepper to the pan. Cook for another 4 minutes. Stir well so that the spinach begins to fall apart and is incorporated into the mixture.
6. Remove the pan from the heat and add the cheese. Stir the mixture until the cheese is melted.
7. Wrap the tortillas in a moist cloth and microwave on high temperature for 1 ½ minutes or until hot.
8. Spoon approximately ⅕ of the mixture into the center of a tortilla. Fold in the ends and then roll the tortilla over the mixture. Roll the tortilla very tightly, then pierce it with a toothpick to hold it together. Repeat with the remaining ingredients until you have five eggrolls. Cover the plate with

plastic wrap and chill for an hour or two. You may chill the eggrolls overnight if you wish.

9. When you are ready to cook the eggrolls, preheat the oven to 425 degrees.

10. Prepare the low-fat avocado-ranch dipping sauce by combining all of the ingredients in a small bowl. Cover and chill this until needed.

11. Spray the entire surface of each of the eggrolls with the oil cooking spray. Arrange the eggrolls on a baking sheet and bake for 17 to 20 minutes or until surface browns and becomes crispy. Turn the eggrolls over about halfway through cooking time.

12. Let the eggrolls cool for a few minutes and then slice each one diagonally lengthwise and arrange on a plate around a small bowl of the dipping sauce. Garnish the dipping sauce with the chopped tomato and onion.

- SERVES 3 OR 4 AS AN APPETIZER.

Nutrition Facts (per serving)

SERVING SIZE—3 HALVES   TOTAL SERVINGS—3.3

	LOW-FAT	ORIGINAL
CALORIES (APPROX.)	480	725
FAT (APPROX.)	12G	42G

• • • •

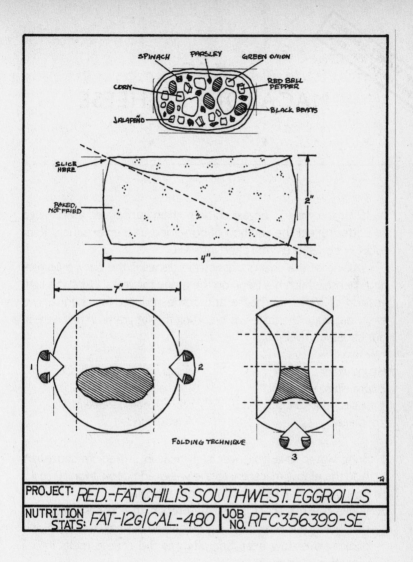

SPINACH PARSLEY GREEN ONION
CORN RED BELL PEPPER
JALAPEÑO BLACK BEANS

SLICE HERE

BAKED, NOT FRIED

2"

4"

7"

1 2

FOLDING TECHNIQUE

3

PROJECT: *RED.-FAT CHILI'S SOUTHWEST. EGGROLLS*

NUTRITION STATS: *FAT-12g/CAL.-480*

JOB NO. *RFC356399-SE*

KFC
MACARONI & CHEESE

In 1991, the world's largest chicken chain introduced a new logo to better reflect the addition of non–fried chicken products. Kentucky Fried Chicken morphed into KFC.

One of the chain's classic side dishes is the tasty macaroni and cheese, which has been on the menu for years. Using the light version of Velveeta cheese and some reduced-fat cheddar, we easily duplicate the taste while cutting the fat grams in half here in our cheesy conversion.

6 cups water
2 cups elbow macaroni
4 ounces Velveeta Light
   cheese

½ cup reduced-fat shredded
   cheddar cheese (2% fat)
2 tablespoons fat-free milk
¼ teaspoon salt

1. Bring water to a boil over high heat in a medium saucepan. Add the elbow macaroni to the water and cook it for 10 to 12 minutes or until tender, stirring occasionally.
2. While the macaroni is boiling, prepare the cheese sauce by combining the remaining ingredients in a small saucepan and cooking over low heat. Stir often as the cheese melts into a smooth consistency.
3. When the macaroni is done, turn off the heat, then use a colander or sieve to strain off the water. Pour the macaroni back into the pan without the water.
4. Pour the cheese sauce over the macaroni and stir until it is well coated. Serve immediately.

- SERVES 6 AS A SIDE DISH.

Nutrition Facts *(per serving)*

SERVING SIZE—5.4 OUNCES   TOTAL SERVINGS—6

	LOW-FAT	ORIGINAL
CALORIES	95	180
FAT	4G	8G

• • • •

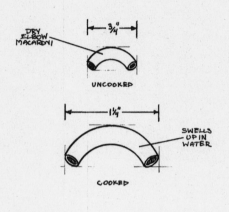

DRY
ELBOW
MACARONI

3/4"

UNCOOKED

1½"

SWELLS
UP IN
WATER

COOKED

PROJECT: *RED.-FAT KFC MACARONI & CHEESE*

NUTRITION
STATS: *FAT- 4 G /CAL.:95*

JOB
NO. *RFKFC99935-MC*

KFC
POTATO SALAD

☆ ✂ ✦ ✎ ◉ ✂ ☞

Sure, KFC's potato salad is good, but have you ever wondered why they don't sell a fat-free version? It really wouldn't be so tough to substitute fat-free mayo for the regular stuff, then just sweeten it up with some sweet pickle relish and sugar. Throw a few spices in there, some bits of veggies, and the recipe might look something like this:

2 pounds russet potatoes, diced
6 cups water
salt
1 cup fat-free mayonnaise
4 teaspoons sweet pickle relish
4 teaspoons granulated sugar
2 teaspoons minced white onion

2 teaspoons prepared mustard
1 teaspoon vinegar
1 teaspoon minced celery
1 teaspoon diced pimentos
½ teaspoon shredded carrot
¼ teaspoon dried parsley
¼ teaspoon ground black pepper
dash salt

1. Lightly peel the potatoes (you don't have to get all of the skin off) then chop them into bite-size pieces (approximately ½-inch cubes) and boil the pieces in 6 cups of boiling, salted water for 7 to 10 minutes. The potato chunks should be tender, yet slightly tough in the middle when done. Drain and rinse the potatoes with cold water.
2. In a medium bowl, combine the remaining ingredients and whisk until smooth.
3. Pour the drained potatoes into a large bowl. Pour the dressing

over the potatoes and mix until all of the potato pieces are well coated.

4. Cover and chill for at least 4 hours. Overnight is best.

- SERVES 8 AS A SIDE DISH.

Nutrition Facts *(per serving)*

SERVING SIZE—5.6 OUNCES   TOTAL SERVINGS—8

	LOW-FAT	ORIGINAL
CALORIES	90	230
FAT	0G	14G

• • • •

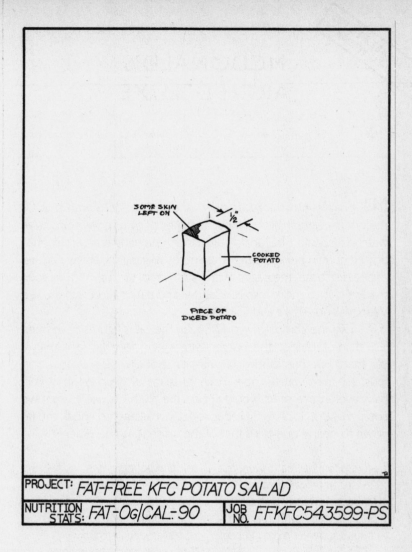

SOME SKIN
LEFT ON

½"

COOKED
POTATO

PIECE OF
DICED POTATO

PROJECT: *FAT-FREE KFC POTATO SALAD*

NUTRITION STATS: *FAT-0g/CAL.-90*

JOB NO. *FFKFC543599-PS*

157

TOP SECRET RECIPES
REDUCED-FAT VERSION OF

MCDONALD'S ARCH DELUXE

☆　　✄　　✿　　✎　　◉　　✂　　☞

McDonald's introduced its new sandwich in 1996 with a $200 million marketing blitz aimed at winning over grown-ups. We watched Ronald McDonald golf, dance, and hang out with sophisticated human beings, rather than his usual gang of creepy dancing puppets. These messages were supposed to tug at the adult market lost to more inspired sandwich creations from chains like Wendy's and Arby's and Carl's Jr.

Did the campaign work? So far, the sales figures have been less than stellar for the burger with even more fat in it than a Big Mac. But the sandwich, with its specially developed Dijon mustard–mayo sauce, does have its share of devoted fans. Perhaps even more of us would get on the Arch Deluxe team if we could make a clone using reduced-fat ingredients to knock the fat down to nearly one-third that of the original, as I have here.

1 tablespoon fat-free mayonnaise	salt and pepper
½ teaspoon brown mustard (French's Hearty Deli is good)	1 slice fat-free American cheese
1 sesame seed hamburger bun	1 large tomato slice
¼ pound super lean ground beef (7% fat)	1 to 2 lettuce leaves, chopped
	½ tablespoon ketchup
	2 tablespoons chopped onion

1. In a small bowl, mix together the mayonnaise and the brown mustard. Set this mixture aside.
2. Grill the face of each of the buns on a griddle or frying pan over medium heat.
3. Roll the ground beef into a ball and pat it out until it's approxi-

mately the same diameter as the bun. You can freeze this patty before you cook it just like the restaurant chain does. This will also make it stay together better when it cooks.

4. Cook the meat on a hot griddle or frying pan for about 5 minutes per side until done. Be sure to lightly salt and pepper each side of the patty.

5. Build the burger in the following order, from the bottom up:

ON BOTTOM BUN
beef patty   *tomato slice*
American cheese slice   *lettuce*

ON TOP BUN
mayo/mustard   *onion*
ketchup

6. Slap the top of the sandwich onto the bottom and serve. Microwave sandwich on high for 15 seconds if you like the sandwich hotter.

• MAKES 1 SANDWICH.

TIDBITS

If you'd like to add bacon to the sandwich, as you can order with the original, just cook a piece of turkey bacon sprinkled with coarsely ground black pepper. Break the bacon in half and place each half of the bacon side by side onto the bottom bun before stacking on the beef patty.

Nutrition Facts (per serving)

SERVING SIZE—1 BURGER		TOTAL SERVINGS—1
	LOW-FAT	ORIGINAL
CALORIES	430	550
FAT	11G	31G

WITH BACON:

Nutrition Facts (per serving)

SERVING SIZE—1 SANDWICH   TOTAL SERVINGS—1

	LOW-FAT	ORIGINAL
CALORIES	450	590
FAT	13.5G	34G

• • • •

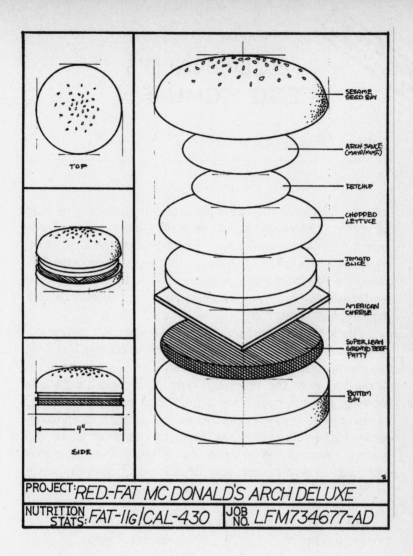

TOP

SIDE

4"

SESAME
SEED BUN

ARCH SAUCE
(MAYO/MUS.)

KETCHUP

CHOPPED
LETTUCE

TOMATO
SLICE

AMERICAN
CHEESE

SUPER LEAN
GROUND BEEF
PATTY

BOTTOM
BUN

PROJECT:	*RED.-FAT MC DONALD'S ARCH DELUXE*
NUTRITION STATS:	*FAT-11g / CAL-430*

JOB NO. *LFM734677-AD*

MCDONALD'S
EGG MCMUFFIN

Like the Big Mac, the idea for this breakfast product came from an inspired McDonald's franchisee goofing around with ingredients in the kitchen—in this case, English muffins and a cylindrical egg mold. It was in 1977 that the world's largest burger chain unveiled the Egg McMuffin to a ravenous America on the go: the eat-breakfast-while-driving, morning rush hour workforce with the spill-proof coffee mugs.

Back then, concerns with fat intake were not big on our minds or in the news, so the 12 grams of fat per Egg McMuffin was disregarded. But if you've had your share of greasy breakfast sandwiches over the years and have a little extra time one morning, give this cool clone a test. Using egg substitute (egg whites) and fat-free American cheese, you can still create that signature Mickey D's taste while cutting the fat down to just 2.5 grams per sandwich. Now when you eat two of these you won't make such a dent in your daily fat allotment before the sun is barely up.

1 English muffin	1 slice Canadian bacon
1/4 cup egg substitute	1 slice fat-free American
salt	cheese

1. Split the English muffin and toast it or grill the faces until brown in a hot pan set over medium heat. Keep the pan hot.
2. Find a shallow can—such as an 8-ounce sliced pineapple can—that has the same diameter as the English muffin. Cut off both ends of the can and thoroughly clean it. Spray a

coating of nonstick spray on the inside of the can, and place it into the hot pan so that it heats up.

3. When the can is hot, spray more nonstick spray over the surface of the pan, and pour the egg substitute into the can. Salt the egg.

4. Place the slice of Canadian bacon into the same pan to heat up while the egg cooks.

5. When the egg seems to be firming up on top, use a knife to scrape around the edge of the can to help release the egg. Carefully pull the can off the egg, then flip the egg over and cook it for an additional minute or so.

6. Build the sandwich by first placing the slice of American cheese on the bottom half of the English muffin.

7. Place the egg on top of the cheese.

8. Stack the Canadian bacon on the egg.

9. Top the sandwich off with the top half of the English muffin.

10. Microwave the sandwich for 10 to 15 seconds until warm, and serve immediately.

• MAKES 1 SANDWICH.

TIDBITS

You can also purchase a device similar to what McDonald's uses to cook the eggs. It is a handle that has 2 to 4 circular molds at the end to hold the egg while it cooks. This can be used instead of a can, but it ain't as cheap!

Nutrition Facts *(per serving)*
SERVING SIZE—1 SANDWICH   TOTAL SERVINGS—1

	LOW-FAT	ORIGINAL
CALORIES	217	290
FAT	2.5G	12G

• • • •

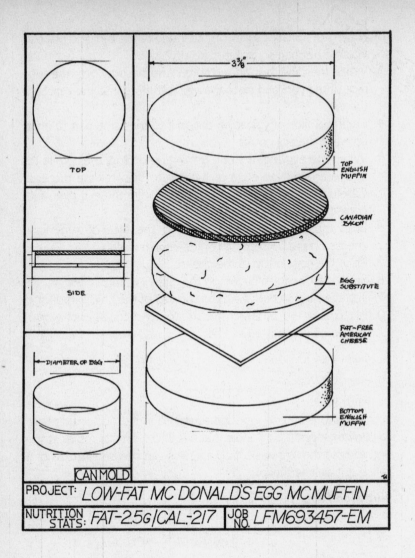

TOP

SIDE

DIAMETER OF EGG

CAN MOLD

TOP ENGLISH MUFFIN

CANADIAN BACON

EGG SUBSTITUTE

FAT-FREE AMERICAN CHEESE

BOTTOM ENGLISH MUFFIN

3⅜"

PROJECT: *LOW-FAT MC DONALD'S EGG MC MUFFIN*

NUTRITION STATS: *FAT-2.5G/CAL.-217*   JOB NO. *LFM693457-EM*

TOP SECRET RECIPES
REDUCED-FAT VERSION OF

OLIVE GARDEN CHICKEN PARMIGIANA SANDWICH

☆   ✄   💣   ✏   ◉   ✂   ☞

Chicken parmigiana is delicious, but who needs all the fat that comes from the traditional process of breading and panfrying the chicken breast in hot oil? Olive Garden's delicious chicken parmigiana sandwich was the perfect product for a reduced-fat clone using a special baking technique for the chicken to replace the greasy frying. Even when we use regular provolone cheese in this recipe, our conversion comes out to around half the fat of the original, which has been filling the bellies of Olive Garden customers since 1995. And there won't be any hot oil splattering your arm.

MARINARA SAUCE

1 ¼ cups tomato puree
    (1 10½-ounce can)
1 teaspoon granulated sugar
1 small clove garlic, minced
½ cup canned, diced tomatoes

¼ teaspoon salt
¼ teaspoon dried oregano
¼ teaspoon dried basil
⅛ teaspoon pepper
¼ teaspoon lemon juice

4 skinless chicken breast fillets
½ cup all-purpose flour
½ cup egg substitute

½ cup Italian-style bread
    crumbs
olive oil cooking spray

4 Italian or sourdough sandwich
    rolls

½ cup shredded provolone
    cheese

1. Combine the ingredients for the marinara sauce in a small or medium saucepan over high heat. When mixture begins to boil, reduce heat to low and simmer for 45 minutes.
2. Prepare chicken by first cutting each breast in half. Fold a piece of plastic wrap around one piece of chicken and pound flat (to about ¼ inch thick) with a mallet. The chicken should be slightly larger in diameter than the sandwich rolls. Repeat with the remaining pieces of chicken.
3. Put the flour, egg substitute, and bread crumbs into 3 separate small bowls. Drop each piece of chicken, 1 at a time, first into the flour, then into the egg, and then coat each thoroughly with the bread crumbs.
4. Preheat oven to 450 degrees.
5. Spray a baking sheet with a generous coating of cooking spray. Place each piece of chicken on the coated baking sheet, then spray the surface of each piece with the cooking spray. Bake for 20 minutes or until the chicken begins to brown.
6. Toast or grill the faces of each roll until light brown.
7. Build each sandwich by first placing one piece of chicken on the bottom half of a roll. Position the chicken slightly off to one side on the roll. Spoon about 1½ tablespoons marinara sauce onto the chicken. Sprinkle a couple teaspoons of the provolone over the sauce. Stack another piece of chicken on the first, with this piece stacked over to the other side of the roll, but also slightly overlapping the first piece. Spread sauce and cheese on this piece as well.
8. Top off the sandwich with the top half of the roll, and serve. Repeat the process to build the remaining sandwiches.

- MAKES 4 SANDWICHES.

Nutrition Facts (per serving)

SERVING SIZE—1 SANDWICH   TOTAL SERVINGS—4

	LOW-FAT	ORIGINAL
CALORIES (APPROX.)	553	631
FAT (APPROX.)	11G	21G

• • • •

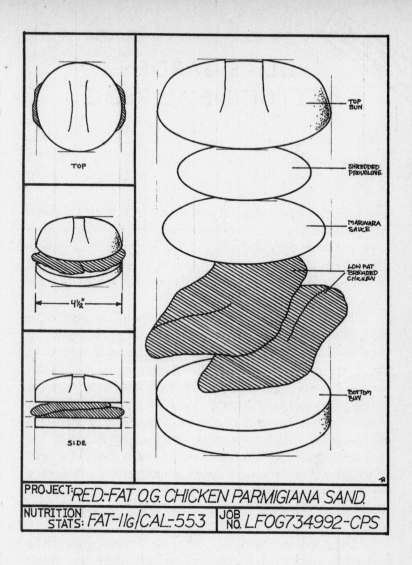

TOP

SIDE

4½"

TOP BUN

SHREDDED PROVOLONE.

MARINARA SAUCE

LOW FAT BREADED CHICKEN

BOTTOM BUN

PROJECT: *RED.-FAT O.G. CHICKEN PARMIGIANA SAND.*

NUTRITION STATS: *FAT-11g/CAL.-553*   JOB NO. *LFOG734992-CPS*

OLIVE GARDEN
FETTUCINE ALFREDO

☆   ✄   💣   ✎   ◉   ✂   ☞

This is a classic Italian dish, but with cheese and cream and butter in the traditional version, you can get a whopping seventy grams of fat in a single plateful. For this conversion, we'll replace those fatty ingredients with substitutes such as evaporated skim milk, fat-free milk, Butter Buds, and a great cheeselike substance made from straining yogurt with a coffee filter.

To easily prepare this useful ingredient, we'll use a technique that I picked up from watching Graham Kerr, the once–galloping gourmet. Graham loves to use this yogurt cheese in many of his low-fat dishes that require a creamy white sauce, traditionally made with fatty foodstuffs. This fat-free substitute is made by straining the whey from the yogurt with a coffee filter. You simply place a filter into a large strainer or metal steamer basket in a covered saucepan. Pour the yogurt into the filter, and let this sit covered overnight in the refrigerator. As the hours tick by, the whey slowly drips from the yogurt, leaving a thick, creamy substance in the filter. The liquid in the bottom of the pan is chucked out, and you measure the yogurt cheese left in the coffee filter for the recipe.

Using this technique, we can shave something like forty-nine grams of fat off the traditional recipe for fettucine alfredo presented at the country's largest Italian restaurant chain. This recipe makes two way-huge dinner-size entrées like they serve at the restaurant, though you might rather divide this up as four more modestly portioned servings.

1 cup strained yogurt (see above)
2 tablespoons cornstarch
1 cup evaporated skim milk
½ teaspoon olive oil
1 large clove garlic, minced
½ cup grated Parmesan cheese
½ cup fat-free milk

1 tablespoon Butter Buds
  Sprinkles
¼ teaspoon salt
⅛ teaspoon ground black
  pepper
4 to 5 quarts water
12-ounce box fettucine pasta

1. Combine the strained yogurt with the cornstarch in a medium bowl. Stir until smooth. Add the evaporated skim milk. Set aside.

2. Heat the oil in a medium saucepan over medium heat. When the oil is hot, add the garlic and sauté for about a minute. Don't cook the garlic long enough that it begins to brown.

3. Add the yogurt mixture to the saucepan and stir. Add remaining ingredients, except the water and pasta, to the saucepan and continue to heat over medium/low heat. If it begins to boil, turn heat to low and simmer, stirring often.

4. As the sauce heats, bring 5 to 6 quarts of water to a rolling boil in a large pot or saucepan. Add the pasta to the boiling water and stir. Return water to a boil, and cook uncovered for 12 to 15 minutes or until pasta is mostly tender but slightly tough (al dente). Strain.

5. Toss pasta and sauce together in a large bowl and serve.

- Serves 2 as a large, restaurant-size portion (or serves 4 as a standard-size entrée).

Nutrition Facts (per serving)
Serving size—4 cups   Total servings—2

	Low-Fat	Original
Calories (approx.)	1035	1236
Fat (approx.)	18g	67g

• • • •

TOP SECRET RECIPES
REDUCED-FAT VERSION OF

OLIVE GARDEN ZUPPA TOSCANA

☆　✂　●　✎　◉　✂　☞

It's the white, creamy broth in the original version of this delicious soup that adds unnecessary fat grams. By replacing the fat-filled dairy ingredients from the original with fat-free milk and chicken broth, and by using lean Italian turkey sausage, we can whack around fifteen grams off the original version.

½ pound hot Italian lean turkey
　　sausage (2 large links)
3 cups fat-free chicken broth
3 cups fat-free milk
2 tablespoons minced onion
1 tablespoon Hormel Real Bacon
　　Pieces

¼ teaspoon salt
dash of crushed red pepper
　　flakes
1 medium russet potato
2 cups chopped kale

1. Grill or sauté the sausage until cooked.
2. Combine the chicken broth, milk, onion, bacon pieces, salt, and pepper flakes in a medium saucepan over medium/high heat.
3. Quarter the potato lengthwise, then cut into ¼-inch slices. Add to the saucepan. When mixture begins to boil, reduce heat and simmer for 30 minutes.
4. Cut the sausage at an angle into ¼-inch-thick slices. Add the sausage to the saucepan. Simmer for 1 hour or until potato slices begin to soften.
5. Add the kale to the soup and simmer for an additional 10 to 15 minutes or until potatoes are soft.

• SERVES 3.

Nutrition Facts *(per serving)*

SERVING SIZE—1 ½ CUPS   TOTAL SERVINGS—3

	LOW-FAT	ORIGINAL
CALORIES (APPROX.)	196	275
FAT (APPROX.)	4.5G	19G

• • • •

TOP SECRET RECIPES
REDUCED-FAT VERSION OF

OTIS SPUNKMEYER
CHOCOLATE CHIP MUFFINS

☆　　🐛　　💣　　🖉　　🌑　　✂　　☞

In Cayce, South Carolina, Otis Spunkmeyer muffins are manufactured with state-of-the-art robotic equipment that would make R2-D2 jealous. The amazing machines do everything from packaging 130 muffins per minute to sealing up the cartons ready for a quick shipment to stores across the country.

This custom Top Secret Recipes reduced-fat clone version uses unsweetened applesauce to keep the muffin moist and to help replace unnecessary fat.

¾ cup granulated sugar
⅔ cup unsweetened applesauce
¼ cup egg substitute
¼ cup vegetable oil
½ teaspoon salt
¾ teaspoon vanilla

1 teaspoon baking soda
½ cup low-fat buttermilk
2 cups all-purpose flour
2 teaspoons baking powder
½ cup mini chocolate chips

1. Preheat oven to 325 degrees.
2. In a large bowl, mix together sugar, applesauce, egg substitute, oil, salt, vanilla, and baking soda. Add buttermilk and blend well.
3. In a separate bowl, sift together the flour and baking powder. Add the dry ingredients to the wet, and mix well with an electric mixer. Add half of the chocolate chips to the batter, and fold them in by hand.
4. To bake the muffins, use a "Texas-size" muffin pan lined with large muffin cups. You may also bake the muffins without the cups; just be sure to grease the pan well with cooking spray. (If you use a regular-size muffin pan, which also works fine, your

cooking time will be a few minutes less and your yield will double.) Fill the cups halfway with batter.

5. Sprinkle the remaining chocolate chips over the tops of each cup of batter. That will be about $\frac{1}{2}$ tablespoon of chips per muffin (or a scant teaspoon of chips if you make the regular-size muffins).

6. Bake the muffins for 20 to 24 minutes or until brown on top (16 to 20 minutes for regular-size muffins). Remove the muffins from the oven and allow them to cool for about 30 minutes. Then put the muffins in a sealed container or resealable plastic bag.

• MAKES 8 "TEXAS-SIZE" MUFFINS (OR 16 REGULAR-SIZE MUFFINS).

Nutrition Facts *(per serving)*

SERVING SIZE—$\frac{1}{2}$ MUFFIN   TOTAL SERVINGS—16

	LOW-FAT	ORIGINAL
CALORIES	160	240
FAT	5.5G	13G

• • • •

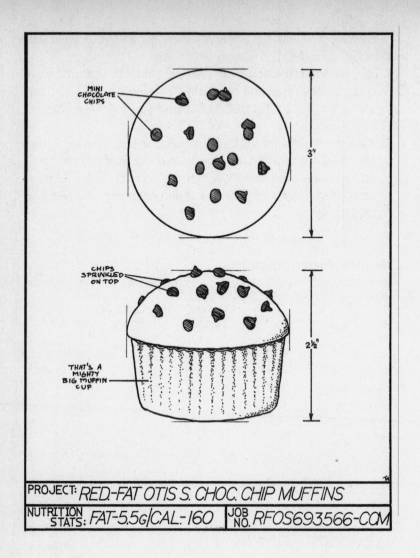

MINI CHOCOLATE CHIPS

3"

CHIPS SPRINKLED ON TOP

THAT'S A MIGHTY BIG MUFFIN CUP

2½"

PROJECT: *RED-FAT OTIS S. CHOC. CHIP MUFFINS*

NUTRITION STATS: *FAT-5.5g/CAL.-160*   JOB NO. *RFOS693566-CCM*

TOP SECRET RECIPES
REDUCED-FAT VERSION OF

OTIS SPUNKMEYER
WILD BLUEBERRY MUFFINS

☆   ✂   💣   ✏   🎱   ✂   ☞

After baking the big 'ol muffins, Otis Spunkmeyer freezes them so that they stay fresh on the way to the stores. Vendors thaw out the tasty baked goodies before displaying them on their shelves. Even after the muffins reach room temperature, they still have a very impressive shelf life of twenty-one days.

You can also freeze the muffins you make with this reduced-fat clone recipe. Just wait until they cool, then wrap the muffins in plastic wrap, and toss them in the freezer. And remember, the shelf life of your version without preservatives will be much less than that of the real McCoy, so dive into those muffins post haste.

1 cup dried blueberries	¾ teaspoon salt
¼ cup water	½ teaspoon vanilla
¾ cup plus 1 tablespoon granulated sugar	1 teaspoon baking soda
	½ cup low-fat buttermilk
⅔ cup unsweetened applesauce	2 cups all-purpose flour
¼ cup egg substitute	2 teaspoons baking powder
¼ cup vegetable oil	fat-free butter-flavored spray

1. Combine blueberries with ¼ cup water in a small, microwave-safe bowl. Zap blueberries in the microwave on 50% power for 2 minutes, stir, cover with plastic wrap, then set aside.
2. Preheat oven to 325 degrees.
3. In a large bowl, mix together ¾ cup of sugar, applesauce, egg substitute, oil, salt, vanilla, and baking soda. Add buttermilk and blend well.
4. In a separate bowl, sift together the flour and baking powder.

Add the dry ingredients to the wet, and mix well with an electric mixer.

5. Add 1 tablespoon of sugar to the blueberries, then add them to the batter and fold in by hand with as few strokes as possible.

6. To bake the muffins, use a "Texas-size" muffin pan lined with large muffin cups. You may also bake the muffins without the cups; just be sure to grease the pan well with cooking spray. (If you use a regular-size muffin pan, which also works fine, your cooking time will be a few minutes less, and your yield will double.) Fill the cups halfway with batter.

7. Spray a couple of squirts of fat-free butter-flavored spray over the top of each portion of batter.

8. Bake the muffins for 20 to 24 minutes or until brown on top (16 to 20 minutes for regular-size muffins). Remove the muffins from the oven, and allow them to cool for about 30 minutes. Then put the muffins in a sealed container or resealable plastic bag.

• MAKES 8 "TEXAS-SIZE" MUFFINS (OR 16 REGULAR-SIZE MUFFINS).

Nutrition Facts (per serving)

SERVING SIZE—½ MUFFIN   TOTAL SERVINGS—16

	LOW-FAT	ORIGINAL
CALORIES	165	210
FAT	4G	11G

• • • •

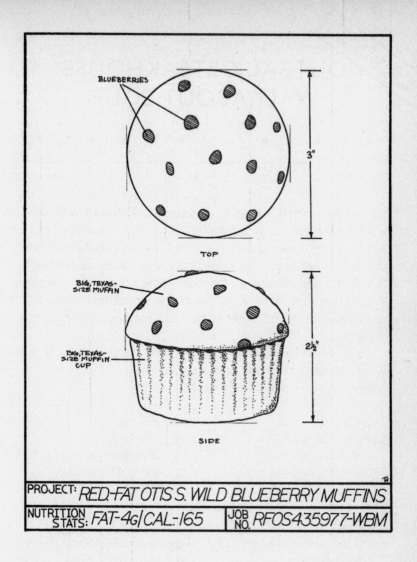

BLUEBERRIES

3"

TOP

BIG, TEXAS-
SIZE MUFFIN

BIG, TEXAS-
SIZE MUFFIN
CUP

2½"

SIDE

| PROJECT: | *RED.-FAT OTIS S. WILD BLUEBERRY MUFFINS* |
| NUTRITION STATS: | *FAT-4G/CAL.-165* | JOB NO. | *RFOS435977-WBM* |

OUTBACK STEAKHOUSE WALKABOUT SOUP

☆   ⚘   ✴   ✎   ◉   ✂   ☞

Restaurateurs Chris Sullivan, Robert Basham, and Timothy Gannon knew they wanted an Australian theme for their new steakhouse and hunkered down to come up with a name. Robert's wife Beth pulled out her lipstick and started writing names on a mirror. "Outback" jumped out as the best name among the choices. When looking for Windex, the group later wondered if it wouldn't have been too much trouble to have just used a pen and a piece of paper.

This creamy onion soup has become a favorite item on the Outback menu. With this formula, you'll get all the flavor of the original with only one-third of the fat.

7 cups water
5 beef bouillon cubes
3 medium-size white onions
2 cups reduced-fat milk (2%)
1 1/2 tablespoons sugar

1 teaspoon salt
1/2 teaspoon pepper
3/4 cup all-purpose flour
1 cup reduced-fat shredded
   cheddar cheese

GARNISH
1/4 cup reduced-fat shredded
   cheddar cheese

1/4 cup Hormel Real Bacon Pieces
1 to 2 green onions, sliced

1. Combine 6 cups of water with the 5 beef bouillon cubes in a large saucepan over medium/high heat. Heat until bouillon cubes have dissolved.
2. Cut the onions into thin slices, then quarter the slices.

3. Add the onions to the broth, reduce heat, and simmer for 15 minutes.
4. Add milk to the pan. Add sugar, salt, and pepper.
5. Combine flour with 1 cup of water in a small bowl or cup, and stir until smooth. Stir the soup while adding this mixture to the pan.
6. Crank heat back up to high, add the reduced-fat cheddar cheese to the pan, and stir. Bring mixture back to boiling. Once the soup begins to boil, reduce heat and simmer for 15 to 20 minutes or until very thick.
7. Spoon 1 cup of soup into a bowl, and garnish with about $\frac{1}{2}$ tablespoon each of cheddar cheese, bacon pieces, and chopped green onion.

• MAKES 8 SERVINGS.

Nutrition Facts (per serving)

SERVING SIZE—1 CUP   TOTAL SERVINGS—8

	LOW-FAT	ORIGINAL
CALORIES (APPROX.)	144	230
FAT (APPROX.)	5.8G	17G

•　•　|　•　•

TOP SECRET RECIPES
LOW-FAT VERSION OF

OUTBACK STEAKHOUSE CAESAR SALAD DRESSING

The salad dressings are made fresh in each Outback Steakhouse from authentic ingredients, including olive oil from Italy's Tuscany region and Parmesan cheese that comes from eighty-pound wheels rolled in from Parma, Italy.

Salad dressings are usually one of the most fat-contributing components in your meal, but with a few tricks, we can clone Outback's delicious salad dressing with only two grams of fat per serving.

1 cup fat-free mayonnaise
1/3 cup water
1/4 cup egg substitute
1/4 cup grated Parmesan
   cheese
1 1/2 tablespoons lemon
   juice

1 tablespoon anchovy paste
2 cloves garlic, pressed
1/2 teaspoon salt
1/2 teaspoon coarsely ground
   pepper
1/4 teaspoon dried parsley flakes,
   crushed fine

1. Combine all ingredients in a medium bowl. Use an electric mixer to beat ingredients for about 1 minute.
2. Cover the dressing and chill it for several hours so that flavors can develop.

• MAKES 1 1/2 CUPS.

Nutrition Facts (per serving)

SERVING SIZE—¼ CUP   TOTAL SERVINGS—6

	LOW-FAT	ORIGINAL
CALORIES (APPROX.)	51	331
FAT (APPROX.)	2G	35G

• • • •

OUTBACK STEAKHOUSE
ALICE SPRINGS CHICKEN

☆　　🌂　　💣　　🖊　　🎱　　✂　　☞

Always a popular choice since the very beginning of this 517-unit steakhouse chain in 1988, the Alice Springs Chicken entrée would not likely be part of any low-fat diet. This marinated chicken breast is covered with honey mustard and bacon. Then the entrée is baked until the cheese on top is all melted and drippy. Add it up, and you've got yourself around forty-four grams of fat in just one serving.

We can cut the fat by more than half using fat-free and low-fat ingredients, plus some delicious-yet-low-fat turkey bacon (I recommend Butterball brand). Tastes just like the original without the guilt. Or the tip.

MARINADE
2 cups water
1 1/2 teaspoons salt
1/2 teaspoon liquid smoke
1/4 teaspoon ground black pepper

1/4 teaspoon onion powder
1/4 teaspoon garlic powder
1/4 teaspoon paprika

4 skinless chicken breast fillets

FAT-FREE HONEY MUSTARD SAUCE
1/2 cup fat-free
   mayonnaise
1/2 cup honey

2 tablespoons Grey Poupon Dijon
   mustard
2 teaspoons white vinegar

8 slices turkey bacon
salt
ground black pepper
paprika
2 cups sliced mushrooms
    (10 to 12 mushrooms)

1 tablespoon butter
2 cups reduced-fat shredded
    Colby and Monterey Jack
    cheese
2 teaspoons minced fresh
    parsley

1. Combine the marinade ingredients in a medium bowl. Add all 4 chicken breasts to the marinade in a covered container or resealable plastic bag, and chill for 3 to 4 hours.

2. Combine the mayonnaise, honey, Dijon mustard, and vinegar in a small bowl. Stir well until smooth. Chill.

3. When chicken has marinated, preheat barbecue grill to high heat.

4. As barbecue preheats, prepare turkey bacon by frying it in a skillet over medium heat until done. Remove the bacon from the skillet to a plate lined with paper, which helps soak up excess fat. The bacon can sit here until it is time to assemble the dish.

5. Spray a light coating of nonstick oil cooking spray over the surface of each chicken breast. Sprinkle both sides of each chicken breast with salt, pepper, and paprika, and then grill for 7 to 10 minutes on each side. Preheat oven to 375 degrees.

6. As chicken grills, prepare mushrooms by heating up a medium skillet over medium/high heat. Add 1 tablespoon of butter to the pan. When the butter has melted, add the mushrooms, along with a little salt and pepper. Sauté the mushrooms for 10 to 15 minutes or until they become cooked through and light brown. If the mushrooms finish before the chicken, just turn the heat to the lowest setting until you are ready to assemble the dish.

7. When chicken is cooked, transfer the chicken breast fillets to a large baking dish. Slather the top surface of each breast with a generous portion of the honey mustard sauce. Stack two slices of bacon, crosswise, on top of each breast.

8. Quarter the mushrooms and stack a portion on top of the

bacon on each chicken breast. Carefully pour about ½ cup of the Colby/Monterey Jack cheese blend over each of the chicken breasts.

9. Bake chicken in the preheated oven for 7 to 12 minutes or until cheese is melted.

10. Sprinkle each with about ½ teaspoon of fresh minced parsley. Serve with additional honey mustard sauce on the side.

- SERVES 4 AS AN ENTRÉE.

Nutrition Facts *(per serving)*

SERVING SIZE—1 PORTION   TOTAL SERVINGS—4

	LOW-FAT	ORIGINAL
CALORIES (APPROX.)	603	838
FAT (APPROX.)	19G	44G

• • • •

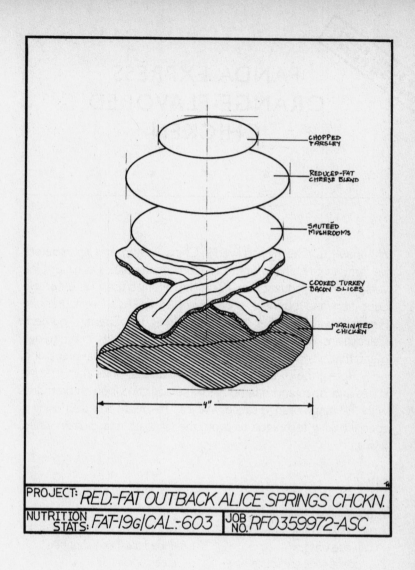

CHOPPED
PARSLEY

REDUCED-FAT
CHEESE BLEND

SAUTEED
MUSHROOMS

COOKED TURKEY
BACON SLICES

MARINATED
CHICKEN

4"

PROJECT: *RED.-FAT OUTBACK ALICE SPRINGS CHCKN.*

NUTRITION
STATS: *FAT-19g/CAL.-603*

JOB
NO. *RFO359972-ASC*

TOP SECRET RECIPES
REDUCED-FAT VERSION OF

PANDA EXPRESS ORANGE-FLAVORED CHICKEN

☆　　　🐝　　　💣　　　🖊　　　🎱　　　✂　　　☞

Andrew J. C. Cherng had lived in China, Taiwan, and Japan before he came to the United States to study mathematics at Baker University. After graduation in 1973, this brainiac used his extensive education and business savvy to open an Asian restaurant in Pasadena with his father, Master Chef Ming Tsai Cherng. Southern Californians went crazy for the Panda Inn and its cutting-edge menu that blended the styles of Szechwan and Mandarin cooking.

Today, the chain includes more than 320 units in thirty-two states and Japan and is famous for the addictive fried chicken dish with the tangy orange sauce. We can re-create this dish using a special baking technique to avoid the fat that's unavoidable when frying.

SAUCE

1½ cups water
2 tablespoons orange juice
1 cup packed dark brown sugar
⅓ cup rice vinegar
2½ tablespoons soy sauce
¼ cup plus 1 teaspoon lemon juice
1 teaspoon minced water chestnuts

½ teaspoon minced fresh ginger
¼ teaspoon minced garlic
1 rounded teaspoon chopped green onion
¼ teaspoon crushed red pepper flakes
5 teaspoons cornstarch
2 teaspoons arrowroot

CHICKEN

4 skinless chicken breast fillets	¼ cup egg substitute
½ cup ice water	1 cup self-rising flour
	¼ teaspoon salt

vegetable oil cooking spray

1. Combine all of the sauce ingredients—except the cornstarch and arrowroot—in a small saucepan over high heat. Stir often while bringing mixture to a boil. When sauce reaches a boil, remove it from heat and allow it to cool a bit, uncovered.

2. Slice chicken breasts into bite-size chunks. Remove exactly 1 cup of the marinade from the pan and pour it over the chicken in a large resealable plastic bag or other container that allows the chicken to be completely covered with the marinade. Chicken should marinate for at least a couple hours. Cover remaining sauce and leave it to cool until the chicken is ready.

3. When chicken has marinated, preheat your oven to 475 degrees.

4. Combine cornstarch with arrowroot in a small bowl, then add 3 tablespoons of water. Stir until cornstarch and arrowroot have dissolved. Pour this mixture into the sauce, and set the pan over high heat. When sauce begins to bubble and thicken, cover and remove from heat.

5. Beat the ice water and egg together in a medium bowl. In another medium bowl, combine the flour and salt.

6. Line a baking sheet with foil. Spray foil with a generous coating of oil cooking spray.

7. First dip each piece of chicken into the flour, then into the egg mixture, and finally back into the flour. Arrange the coated chicken pieces on the baking sheet. When all of the chicken is positioned on the baking sheet, spray a coating of the oil cooking spray over the top of the chicken.

8. Bake the chicken for 4 to 6 minutes or until it begins to brown on top. Turn the oven up to high broil for 2 to 3 minutes or until chicken has browned and has a crispy coating.

9. As the chicken cooks, reheat the sauce left covered on the stove. Stir it occasionally.
10. Pour the chicken into a large serving dish. Cover it with the thickened sauce. Stir gently until all of the pieces are well coated.

- SERVES 4.

Nutrition Facts *(per serving)*

SERVING SIZE—1 SLICED CHICKEN BREAST   TOTAL SERVINGS—4

	LOW-FAT	ORIGINAL
CALORIES (APPROX.)	400	580
FAT (APPROX.)	12G	30G

• • • •

TOP SECRET RECIPES
REDUCED-FAT VERSION OF

RAINFOREST CAFE TROPICAL CHICKEN QUARTET

☆   ✌   💣   ✏   ●   ✂   ☞

This item has been on the theme eatery's menu since the first restaurant opened back in 1994. It was called Tortuga Tidbits back then, but as a restaurant spokesperson explains, "No one knew what a Tortuga Tidbit was … neither did we. So last year we changed the name to make it more descriptive of the menu item."

For this low-fat conversion, we'll need to use the Top Secret Recipes version of Rainforest Cafe Reggae spice blend from page 87. The recipe is designed to make a rather unusual yield total of three sandwiches, since the dinner rolls come in packages of twelve.

SPICY REMOULADE SAUCE

¼ cup fat-free mayonnaise
2 teaspoons finely minced fresh
   parsley
1 teaspoon prepared horseradish
1 teaspoon French dressing
1 teaspoon finely minced onion

½ teaspoon finely minced garlic
½ teaspoon Tabasco pepper
   sauce
½ teaspoon Grey Poupon Dijon
   mustard
¼ teaspoon white vinegar

3 skinless chicken breast fillets
oil cooking spray
TSR version of Reggae
   Beat Seasoning (from
   page 87)

6 canned pineapple slices
1 package of 12 homestyle
   dinner rolls
fat-free butter-flavored
   spray

1 1/2 cups shredded lettuce
2 Roma tomatoes, sliced

4 slices fat-free Kraft mozzarella
cheese singles

1. Prepare the spicy remoulade sauce by combining the ingredients in a small bowl. Cover and chill until needed.
2. Preheat barbecue grill to high temperature.
3. Pound the chicken breasts lightly until about 1/2 inch thick. Spray each breast with a light coating of oil cooking spray. Sprinkle a generous portion of Reggae Beat Seasoning clone over one side of each chicken breast. Place each breast, seasoned side down, onto the grill. Sprinkle additional seasoning over the top of each chicken breast. Arrange the pineapple slices on the grill with the chicken. Grill the pineapple slices and chicken for 2 to 3 minutes per side or until done.
4. While chicken cooks, heat up a large skillet over medium heat. Separate the dinner rolls into groups of four.
5. Keeping the rolls attached in groups of four, spray the face of each group of rolls with a light coating of butter-flavored spray, and then grill the faces until golden brown in the hot skillet. Arrange the rolls on three separate plates for assembly.
6. Spread 1 teaspoon of the remoulade sauce onto the faces of the bottom buns. Sprinkle some shredded lettuce onto the sauce, and then place a slice of tomato on each of the 4 rolls per sandwich.
7. When the chicken is done, cut each breast into 4 equal-size pieces. Arrange the chicken onto the lettuce on each sandwich.
8. Cut each slice of cheese into quarters. Arrange a quarter-slice of cheese over the chicken on each sandwich.
9. Cut each pineapple slice in half and position the half on the cheese on each sandwich. That's 4 pineapple halves per 4-roll sandwich.
10. Finish off the sandwich by placing the top half of the group of 4 rolls on each sandwich and serve.

• SERVES 3 AS AN ENTRÉE.

Nutrition Facts *(per serving)*

SERVING SIZE—1 4-ROLL TOTAL SERVINGS—3
  SANDWICH

	LOW-FAT	ORIGINAL
CALORIES (APPROX.)	768	863
FAT (APPROX.)	14G	27G

• • • •

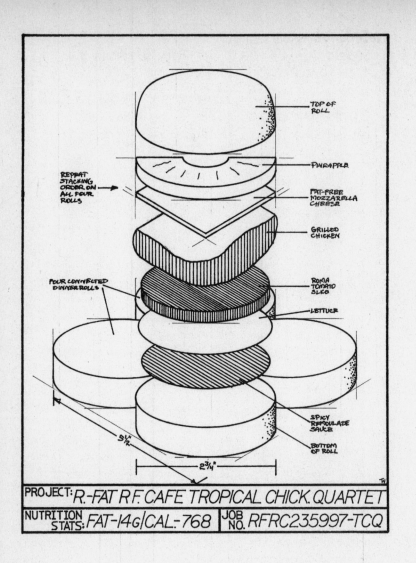

TOP OF ROLL

PINEAPPLE

FAT-FREE MOZZARELLA CHEESE

GRILLED CHICKEN

ROMA TOMATO SLICE

LETTUCE

SPICY REMOULADE SAUCE

BOTTOM OF ROLL

REPEAT STACKING ORDER ON ALL FOUR ROLLS

FOUR CONNECTED DINNER ROLLS

5½"

2¾"

TW

PROJECT: R.-FAT R.F. CAFE TROPICAL CHICK. QUARTET

NUTRITION STATS: FAT-14g/CAL.-768

JOB NO. RFRC235997-TCQ

SCREAMING YELLOW ZONKERS

☆   ✄   💣   ✎   ☯   ✂   ☞

This oddly named popcorn confection gets its yellow color from the butter-flavored popcorn beneath the nearly clear candy coating. We'll use microwave popcorn for this low-fat version, and we'll throw in some real butter and butter flavoring for just the right touch. With this secret formula, we can duplicate the taste of the original with only half the fat.

½ cup light corn syrup
½ cup granulated sugar
¼ cup water
2 tablespoons butter
¾ teaspoon salt

½ teaspoon butter flavoring
¼ teaspoon vanilla extract
1 bag of 94% fat-free microwave
    butter popcorn

1. Combine the corn syrup, sugar, water, butter, and salt in a small saucepan over medium heat. Stir while bringing mixture to a boil, then use a candy thermometer to bring mixture to 300 degrees (in candy making this is known as the hard crack stage).

2. When the candy reaches about 275 degrees, start cooking the popcorn following the directions on the package. You want to time it so that the popcorn is done at approximately the same time as the candy. This way the popcorn will be hot when you pour the candy over it.

3. When the candy has reached the right temperature, remove it from the heat, then add the butter flavoring and vanilla extract. Pour the hot popcorn into a large plastic or glass bowl and quickly pour the candy over it. Stir the popcorn around a bit,

then microwave the bowl on high temperature for 30 seconds. Stir the popcorn again; then, if necessary, microwave it once more for an additional 30 seconds. Stir again. By this time, the popcorn should be very well coated with the candy.

4. Quickly pour the popcorn out onto wax paper and spread it around to cool it.

5. When candy is cool, break it into bite-size pieces. Store it in a sealed container.

- MAKES 12 CUPS.

Nutrition Facts (per serving)

SERVING SIZE—1 CUP   TOTAL SERVINGS—12

	LOW-FAT	ORIGINAL
CALORIES	107	140
FAT	2G	4G

• • • •

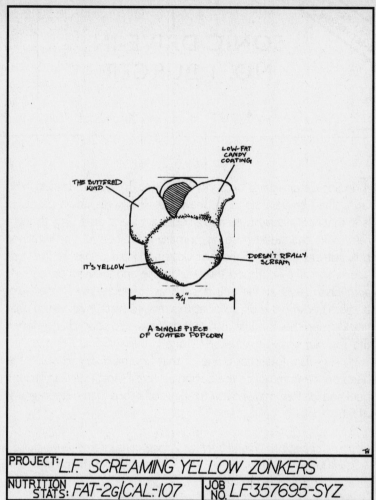

LOW-FAT
CANDY
COATING

THE BUTTERED
KIND

IT'S YELLOW

DOESN'T REALLY
SCREAM

3/4"

A SINGLE PIECE
OF COATED POPCORN

PROJECT: *L.F. SCREAMING YELLOW ZONKERS*

NUTRITION
STATS: *FAT-2g/CAL.-107*

JOB
NO. *LF357695-SYZ*

SONIC DRIVE-IN
NO. 1 BURGER

☆   ✌   ☄   ✏   ☯   ✄   ☞

The Sonic story starts back in 1953, when Troy Smith traded in his failing fried chicken stand in Shawnee, Oklahoma, for a parcel of land that had a steakhouse and a root beer stand on it. Troy thought he'd make the steakhouse his primary operation, but as it turned out, patrons preferred the hot dogs and cold drinks at the root beer stand. Troy dumped the steakhouse and focused on offering additional items at the stand, such as hamburgers. Those hamburgers became the big seller at this revised restaurant, which Troy had dubbed the Top Hat. But that name would soon change when the Top Hat sign was replaced by one that read Sonic Drive-In.

This is a lower-fat clone of that first hamburger, which has been on the menu since the beginning. We'll substitute lean ground beef and fat-free mayonnaise to shear off more than sixteen grams of fat.

¼-pound super lean ground beef (7% fat)
1 large plain white hamburger bun
fat-free butter-flavored spray
salt
ground black pepper

2 teaspoons fat-free mayonnaise
3 dill pickle slices (hamburger slices)
1 tablespoon chopped white onion
⅓ cup chopped lettuce
2 tomato slices

1. Pound the ground beef into a thin circle the same diameter as the bun. Cover with wax paper and freeze.
2. When ready to prepare the burger, preheat a large skillet over medium heat.

3. Spray a light coating of the butter spray over the face of the top and bottom bun. Brown the faces of the bun in the skillet, then remove them and set them aside.
4. Place the beef patty into the skillet, and lightly sprinkle it with salt and pepper. Cook for 3 to 4 minutes per side until done.
5. As the patty cooks, build the burger by first spreading the mayonnaise over the face of the bottom bun.
6. Arrange the pickle slices on the mayonnaise.
7. Sprinkle the chopped onion over the pickles.
8. Arrange the lettuce on the sandwich next.
9. Stack the tomato slices on the lettuce.
10. When the beef is ready, stack it on top of the other condiments, and top off the sandwich with the top bun. If you'd like the sandwich hotter, microwave on high for 10 to 15 seconds.

• MAKES 1 SANDWICH.

Nutrition Facts *(per serving)*

SERVING SIZE—1 SANDWICH   TOTAL SERVINGS—1

	LOW-FAT	ORIGINAL
CALORIES	400	409
FAT	10.5G	26.6G

• • • •

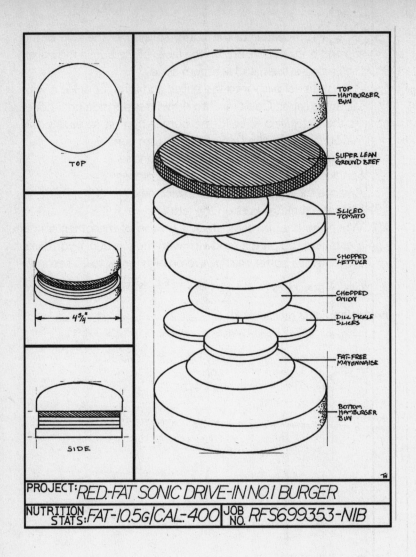

TOP

SIDE

4 3/4"

TOP HAMBURGER BUN

SUPER LEAN GROUND BEEF

SLICED TOMATO

CHOPPED LETTUCE

CHOPPED ONION

DILL PICKLE SLICES

FAT-FREE MAYONNAISE

BOTTOM HAMBURGER BUN

PROJECT: *RED-FAT SONIC DRIVE-IN NO.1 BURGER*

NUTRITION STATS: *FAT-10.5g/CAL-400* **JOB NO.** *RFS699353-N1B*

TOP SECRET RECIPES
REDUCED-FAT VERSION OF

SONIC DRIVE-IN HICKORY BURGER

☆　　✌　　💣　　🖊　　◉　　✂　　☞

Driving through Louisiana in 1953, Troy Smith happened upon a cozy hamburger stand that had installed an intercom system to speed up ordering. Troy adapted the idea for his small chain of burger joints and hired nimble servers to bring the food out to customers quickly. The concept was a smash, with revenues for the chain doubling during the first week. Sonic was cashing in on the growing popularity of the automobile. Customers parked their cars in a stall, rolled down the window, and ordered from a speaker. The food was then brought to the car on a tray by a roller-skating carhop with extraordinary balance.

Today, Sonic has rejuvenated the carhop concept by serving customers the same way as in the '50s; with individual car stalls, speakers, and waitresses on wheels. The company is America's largest drive-in hamburger chain with more than two thousand units rolling in 1999.

¼ pound super lean ground beef (7% fat)
1 large plain white hamburger bun
fat-free butter-flavored spray
salt

ground black pepper
1 tablespoon Kraft Hickory BBQ Sauce
1 tablespoon chopped white onion
⅓ cup chopped lettuce

1. Pound the ground beef into a circle the same diameter as the bun. Cover the meat with wax paper and freeze it.
2. When ready to prepare the burger, preheat a large skillet over medium heat.

3. Spray a light coating of the butter-flavored spray over the face of the top and bottom bun. Brown the faces of the bun in the skillet, then remove it and set it aside.
4. Place the beef patty into the skillet, and lightly sprinkle it with salt and pepper. Cook for 3 to 4 minutes per side until done.
5. As patty cooks, build the burger by first spreading the BBQ sauce over the face of the bottom bun.
6. Sprinkle the chopped onion over the sauce.
7. Arrange the lettuce on the sandwich next.
8. When the beef is ready, stack it on top of the other condiments and top off the sandwich with the top bun. If you'd like the sandwich hotter, microwave on high for 10 to 15 seconds.

• MAKES 1 SANDWICH.

Nutrition Facts *(per serving)*

SERVING SIZE—1 SANDWICH   TOTAL SERVINGS—1

	LOW-FAT	ORIGINAL
CALORIES	400	314
FAT	10.5G	15.7G

• • • •

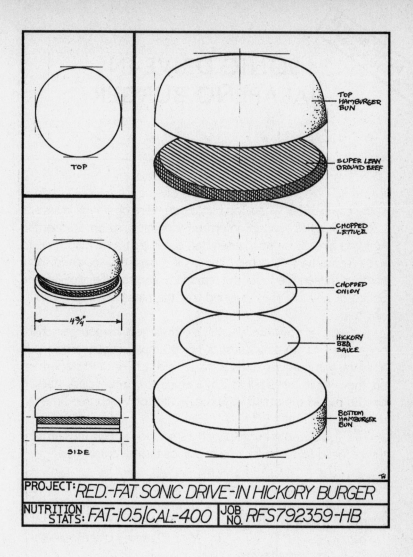

TOP

SIDE

4 3/4"

TOP HAMBURGER BUN

SUPER LEAN GROUND BEEF

CHOPPED LETTUCE

CHOPPED ONION

HICKORY BBQ SAUCE

BOTTOM HAMBURGER BUN

PROJECT: *RED.-FAT SONIC DRIVE-IN HICKORY BURGER*

NUTRITION STATS: *FAT-10.5/CAL-400* **JOB NO.** *RFS792359-HB*

SONIC DRIVE-IN
JALAPEÑO BURGER

☆   ✄   ●   ✎   ◉   ✂   ☞

One day in 1958, when Top Hat chains were operating in several Oklahoma cities, lawyers informed founder Troy Smith that *Top Hat* was already a copyrighted name and that he would have to make some hasty changes. The chain's partners searched for a name that summed up the company motto: "Service at the Speed of Sound." They decided that the name *Sonic* had a spiffy ring to it.

Sonic is now the country's fifth-largest hamburger chain, boasting some amazing statistics. For example, if you were to take all of the hamburger patties Sonic served last year and stack them up, they would be as tall as 2,576 Empire State Buildings stacked one on top of the other. Which guy with too much free time figured that one out?

If you like your burgers with a spicy kick and dig mustard, try this reduced-fat clone for one of Sonic's tastiest creations.

¼ pound super lean ground beef
    (7% fat)
1 large plain white hamburger
    bun
fat-free butter-flavored spray
salt

ground black pepper
1 ½ teaspoons prepared yellow
    mustard
6 to 10 canned jalapeño slices
    (nacho rings)
⅓ cup chopped lettuce

1. Pound the ground beef into a circle the same diameter as the bun. Cover the meat with wax paper and freeze it.
2. When ready to prepare the burger, preheat a large skillet over medium heat.

3. Spray a light coating of the butter spray over the face of the top and bottom bun. Brown the faces of the bun in the skillet, then remove it and set it aside.
4. Place the beef patty into the skillet, and lightly sprinkle it with salt and pepper. Cook for 3 to 4 minutes per side until done.
5. As the patty cooks, build the burger by first spreading the mustard over the face of the bottom bun.
6. Arrange the jalapeño slices on the mustard.
7. Arrange the lettuce on the sandwich next.
8. When the beef is ready, stack it on top of the other condiments and top off the sandwich with the top bun. If you'd like the sandwich hotter, microwave on high for 10 to 15 seconds.

- MAKES 1 SANDWICH.

Nutrition Facts (per serving)
SERVING SIZE—1 SANDWICH   TOTAL SERVINGS—1

	LOW-FAT	ORIGINAL
CALORIES (APPROX.)	400	380
FAT (APPROX.)	10.5G	16G

• • • •

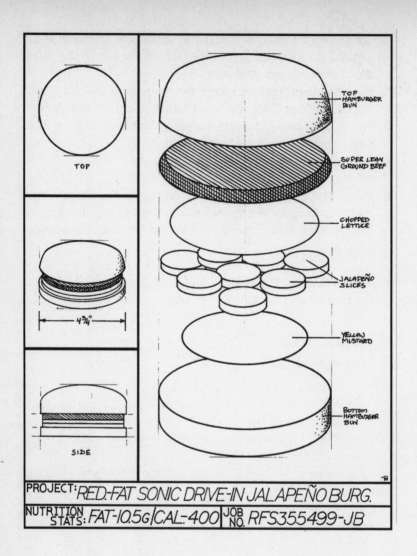

TOP

SIDE

4¾"

TOP
HAMBURGER
BUN

SUPER LEAN
GROUND BEEF

CHOPPED
LETTUCE

JALAPEÑO
SLICES

YELLOW
MUSTARD

BOTTOM
HAMBURGER
BUN

PROJECT: *RED-FAT SONIC DRIVE-IN JALAPEÑO BURG.*

NUTRITION
STATS: *FAT-10.5g* / *CAL-400* JOB
NO. *RFS355499-JB*

TACO BELL
BEEF BURRITO SUPREME

☆　🐝　💣　✎　🎱　✂　☞

How's this for coincidence: Both McDonald's and Taco Bell got their start in San Bernardino, California, in the early '50s. Glen Bell opened a hamburger and hot dog stand called Bell's Drive-In, while the McDonald brothers, Dick and Mac, were just around the corner with their golden arches and speedy drive-up service. "The appearance of another hamburger stand worried me then," says Glen. "I just didn't think there was enough room in town for both of us." Turns out there was enough room—at least for a little while.

In 1962, Glen decided that it was time to offer an alternative to the hamburger stands that were saturating the area, so he opened the first Taco Bell and changed his menu to Mexican food.

Ten years and hundreds of new Taco Bell openings later, the Burrito Supreme hit the menu and became an instant hit. By making this clone version at home, we can reduce the fat to less than one-fifth that of the original.

½ pound super lean ground beef
    (7% fat)
2 tablespoons all-purpose flour
¾ teaspoon salt
¼ teaspoon dried, minced onion
¼ teaspoon paprika
1½ teaspoons chili powder
dash garlic powder
dash onion powder

¼ cup water
1 cup fat-free refried beans
4 10-inch fat-free flour tortillas
1 cup shredded iceberg
    lettuce
½ cup fat-free shredded cheddar
    cheese
1 medium tomato, diced
¼ cup fat-free sour cream

1. In a medium bowl, combine the super lean ground beef with the flour, salt, minced onion, paprika, chili powder, garlic powder, and onion powder. Use your hands to thoroughly incorporate everything into the ground beef.
2. Preheat a skillet over medium/low heat, and add the ground beef mixture to the pan along with the water. Brown the beef mixture for 5 to 6 minutes, using a wooden spoon or spatula to break up the meat as it cooks.
3. Put the refried beans into a microwave-safe container and cover. Heat on high for 2 to 3 minutes or until hot. You may also heat the beans in a small saucepan on the stove over medium/low heat. Stir occasionally, and heat until hot.
4. Using the microwave, heat up 4 10-inch fat-free flour tortillas in a tortilla steamer (or wrapped in a moist cloth or paper towels) for 25 to 30 seconds or until hot.
5. Spread about ¼ cup of refried beans in a 2-inch-wide strip down the center of one tortilla. Don't spread the beans all the way to the edge of the tortilla. Leave a margin of a couple inches so that you can later fold the tortilla.
6. Spread ¼ cup of the beef over the refried beans.
7. Sprinkle ¼ cup of lettuce onto the beef.
8. Sprinkle 2 tablespoons of the fat-free cheese onto the lettuce.
9. Sprinkle 2 tablespoons of diced tomato over the cheese.
10. Finish the burrito by dropping a tablespoon of fat-free sour cream over the other fillings.
11. Fold the left side of the tortilla over the fillings. Fold up the bottom, then fold the right side over, and serve hot. Repeat with the remaining ingredients.

- MAKES 4 BURRITOS.

Nutrition Facts (per serving)
SERVING SIZE—1 BURRITO   TOTAL SERVINGS—4

	LOW-FAT	ORIGINAL
CALORIES	325	503
FAT	4G	22G

• • • •

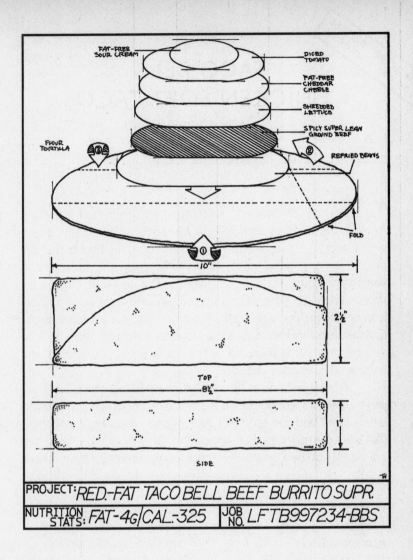

FAT-FREE
SOUR CREAM

DICED
TOMATO

FAT-FREE
CHEDDAR
CHEESE

SHREDDED
LETTUCE

SPICY SUPER LEAN
GROUND BEEF

FLOUR
TORTILLA

REFRIED BEANS

③

②

①

FOLD

10"

2½"

TOP
8½"

1"

SIDE

PROJECT: *RED.-FAT TACO BELL BEEF BURRITO SUPR.*

NUTRITION
STATS: *FAT-4g/CAL.-325*

JOB
NO. *LFTB997234-BBS*

TOP SECRET RECIPES
LOW-FAT VERSION OF

TACO BELL
CHICKEN SOFT TACO

☆　　✌　　💣　　✎　　☯　　✂　　☞

Taco Bell had very little luck with light menu items over the years. In 1983, the Mexican fast-food chain introduced Taco Light, a taco with a fried flour tortilla shell. But the fried flour tortilla that replaced the traditional corn tortilla only made the taco light in weight and color, not in fat or calories. The item was quickly discontinued. In 1995, the chain tried again with Light Line, a selection of several lower-fat menu items that also took a sales digger. Customers who frequented the drive-thru weren't there to lose weight; they were there to ingest some greasy taco meat and handfuls of shredded cheddar.

When we cook at home, though, we'd like to do what we can to make a meal better on the waistline, especially if it takes no extra effort and the food still tastes good. This recipe will show that you can do just that: knock the fat way down—from ten grams to just two grams—without compromising flavor. Check it out.

½ cup water
1 teaspoon soy sauce
1 teaspoon salt
1 teaspoon brown sugar
½ teaspoon onion powder
¼ teaspoon liquid smoke
¼ teaspoon ground black pepper

¼ teaspoon chili powder
2 skinless chicken breast fillets
6 6-inch fat-free flour tortillas
¾ cups shredded iceberg lettuce
½ cup fat-free shredded cheddar
　　cheese
1 medium tomato, diced

1. In a small bowl combine water, soy sauce, salt, brown sugar, onion powder, liquid smoke, black pepper, and chili powder in

a small bowl. Pour the mixture over the chicken breasts and marinate overnight. You can marinate for less time if you wish, but overnight is best.

2. Cook chicken on barbecue or indoor grill over medium/high heat for 5 to 6 minutes per side or until done. Slice chicken into bite-size chunks.

3. Heat the tortillas in a steamer, or wrap them in a moist towel and heat for about 30 seconds in the microwave.

4. Spread about ¼ cup of chicken down the middle of one of the flour tortillas.

5. Sprinkle about 2 tablespoons of lettuce over the chicken.

6. Sprinkle a heaping tablespoon of cheese over the lettuce.

7. Finish the taco by stacking a heaping tablespoon of diced tomato on the cheese, then fold up the edges of the taco, and serve immediately. Repeat with the remaining ingredients.

• MAKES 6 TACOS.

Nutrition Facts (per serving)

SERVING SIZE—1 TACO   TOTAL SERVINGS—6

	LOW-FAT	ORIGINAL
CALORIES	172	213
FAT	2G	10G

• • • •

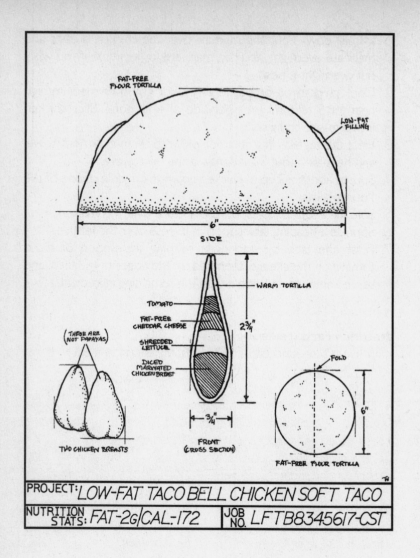

FAT-FREE
FLOUR TORTILLA

LOW-FAT
FILLING

6"

SIDE

WARM TORTILLA

TOMATO

FAT-FREE
CHEDDAR CHEESE

SHREDDED
LETTUCE

DICED
MARINATED
CHICKEN BREAST

2¾"

¾"

FRONT
(CROSS SECTION)

(THESE ARE
NOT PAPAYAS)

TWO CHICKEN BREASTS

FOLD

6"

FAT-FREE FLOUR TORTILLA

PROJECT: *LOW-FAT TACO BELL CHICKEN SOFT TACO*

NUTRITION STATS: *FAT-2g/CAL-172*

JOB NO. *LFTB8345617-CST*

TOP SECRET RECIPES
REDUCED-FAT VERSION OF

T.G.I. FRIDAY'S
BBQ CHICKEN WINGS

☆   ✌   💥   ✐   ☯   ✂   ☞

You've got to hand it to him. Alan Stillman thought that if he opened his own restaurant, it might be a great way to meet the flight attendants who lived in his New York City neighborhood. Not only did the dude follow through on his plan in 1965 with the first T.G.I. Friday's, but today the company is 387 units strong, Alan's rich, and his inspiration is still a popular casual dining spot for delicious finger foods, drinks, lunches, and dinners in an upbeat, festive atmosphere. Nowadays, the chain goes through more than five million chicken wings in a year, serving buffalo wings as well as this variation of the tasty appetizer.

Friday's kitchen came up with a delicious blend of barbecue sauce and apple butter to coat the deep-fried chicken wings. For our reduced-fat clone, we'll re-create the exact taste of the barbecue sauce, but we'll strip the skin from the chicken wings and use a cool baking process that'll cut the fat way down. By the way, I hear flight attendants love wings.

oil nonstick cooking spray
12 chicken wings with skin
½ cup Bull's-Eye or K.C.
    Masterpiece Barbecue Sauce
    (original flavor only)

2 tablespoons apple butter
½ cup flour
1 teaspoon salt
½ teaspoon ground pepper
1 cup milk

1. Preheat the oven on broil.
2. Line a cookie sheet or shallow baking pan with a sheet of aluminum foil. Spray the foil with nonstick spray.
3. Arrange each chicken wing on the foil with the side that has

the most skin on it facing up. Broil the wings for 12 to 14 minutes or until the skin begins to turn light brown and becomes crispy. Remove wings from the oven and let them cool. Turn the oven to 450 degrees.

4. While the wings are broiling, combine the barbecue sauce with the apple butter in a small bowl. Chill the sauce until the wings are ready.

5. Prepare the breading by combining the flour, salt, and pepper in a small bowl. Pour the milk into another small bowl.

6. When you can handle the chicken wings, remove the skin from each one. Throw the skin out.

7. Dip the wings, one at a time, into the breading, then into the milk, and finally back in the breading, so that each one is well coated.

8. Place the wings back onto the baking sheet. Spray a coating of oil spray over each wing so that the breading is completely moistened, and then bake the wings at 450 degrees for 12 minutes. Crank the oven up to broil for 3 to 5 minutes or until the wings begin to brown and become crispy.

9. Remove the wings from the oven. Let them rest for about a minute, then put them into a large plastic container or jar with a lid. Pour a generous amount of sauce over the wings, cover, and gently shake the wings up so that they are all well coated with the sauce. Be careful not to shake too hard or the breading may fall off. Serve immediately.

- SERVES 4 AS AN APPETIZER.

Nutrition Facts (per serving)
SERVING SIZE—3 PIECES   TOTAL SERVINGS—4

	LOW-FAT	ORIGINAL
CALORIES (APPROX.)	150	235
FAT (APPROX.)	6G	16G

• • • •

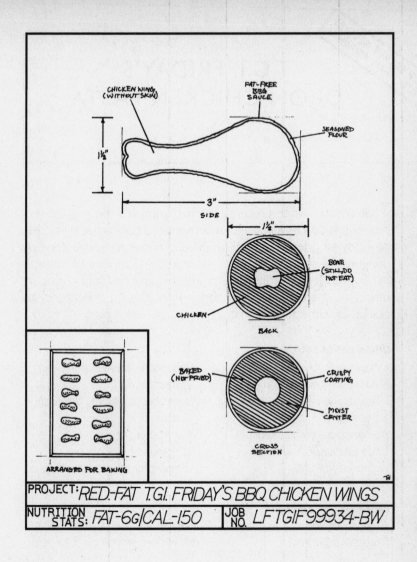

CHICKEN WING
(WITHOUT SKIN)

FAT-FREE
BBQ
SAUCE

SEASONED
FLOUR

1½"

3"

SIDE

1½"

BONE
(STILL DO
NOT EAT)

CHICKEN

BACK

BAKED
(NOT FRIED)

CRISPY
COATING

MOIST
CENTER

CROSS
SECTION

ARRANGED FOR BAKING

PROJECT: *RED-FAT T.G.I. FRIDAY'S BBQ CHICKEN WINGS*

NUTRITION STATS: *FAT-6g/CAL-150*   JOB NO. *LFTGIF99934-BW*

T.G.I. FRIDAY'S
DIJON CHICKEN PASTA

☆　✌　💣　✏　◉　✄　☞

That creamy, white Dijon sauce that smothers the original version of this delicious pasta is luscious indeed but cursed by oodles of flabby fat grams. This can be fixed in our reduced-fat clone by using strained fat-free yogurt—an ingredient apparently inspired by the ancient Mediterranean technique of straining yogurt through a cheesecloth—that adds a thick, creamy consistency to our sauce without adding fat.

DIJON PASTA SAUCE

1 clove garlic, pressed
½ teaspoon olive oil
1 cup strained fat-free
　　yogurt*
2 tablespoons cornstarch
1 cup evaporated skim milk
¼ cup fat-free milk

2 teaspoons Grey Poupon Dijon
　　mustard
2 tablespoons grated Parmesan
　　cheese
¼ teaspoon salt
dash ground black pepper
1½ tablespoons fresh parsley, chopped

CHICKEN SPICE BLEND

2 teaspoons salt
1 teaspoon paprika

½ teaspoon dried thyme
dash or two ground black pepper

fat-free butter-flavored spread or
　　spray
4 skinless chicken breast fillets

1-pound package penne pasta
3 to 4 quarts water

* Make the strained yogurt by pouring a large container of plain yogurt into a coffee filter placed in a metal steamer basket or strainer. Overnight, the liquid whey will drain from the yogurt, leaving a thick, cheeselike substance in the strainer. Measure this thick stuff for the recipe and toss out the liquid.

GARNISH

1 small tomato, diced   *fresh parsley, chopped*

1. Preheat barbecue or stovetop grill to medium/high heat.
2. Prepare pasta sauce by first sautéing the pressed garlic in the olive oil in a medium saucepan. Sauté only for a minute or two over medium heat. Do not let the garlic brown or it will become bitter. Remove pan from heat.
3. Combine strained yogurt with cornstarch in a medium bowl. Add evaporated milk, fat-free milk, and mustard, and mix. Pour mixture into saucepan and place it back over heat. Add Parmesan cheese, salt, and pepper, and stir.
4. When sauce thickens, add parsley and turn heat to low, stirring often.
5. As sauce cooks, prepare the chicken by combining all of the spice blend ingredients in a small bowl. Rub a light coating of butter-flavored spread or spray over each breast, and sprinkle some of the spice blend over both sides of each chicken breast. Cook the chicken on the grill for 4 to 5 minutes per side. Turn the chicken at a 45-degree angle halfway through the cooking time on each side, so that you get crisscrossed grill marks on the surface.
6. While chicken is grilling, prepare pasta by bringing 3 to 4 cups of water to a boil in a large pan. Add pasta to the water and cook for 12 to 15 minutes or until pasta is tender. Strain.
7. Divide strained pasta into four portions on four plates, and pour a generous portion of the sauce over the pasta. Sprinkle some diced tomato over the pasta on each plate. Sprinkle some additional fresh parsley over the pasta.
8. Slice each chicken breast across the grain, and arrange each sliced breast on top of the pasta on each plate, being careful to retain the shape of the chicken breast as you position it.

- SERVES 4 AS AN ENTRÉE.

Nutrition Facts *(per serving)*

SERVING SIZE—1 ENTRÉE   TOTAL SERVINGS—4

	LOW-FAT	ORIGINAL
CALORIES (APPROX.)	730	930
FAT (APPROX.)	8G	45G

• • • •

TOP SECRET RECIPES
REDUCED-FAT VERSION OF

T.G.I. FRIDAY'S POTATO SKINS

☆   ✄   ●   ✎   ◉   ✂   ☞

Thousands of restaurants all over the world now serve this tasty finger food on their appetizer menu, but T.G.I. Friday's is the potato skin king. The restaurant introduced America to the little cheese- and bacon-covered spud boats back in 1974, and the dish quickly took off. As this recipe demonstrates, potato skins can be a great choice for the munchies and don't have to be filled with even half of the traditional fourteen grams of fat per serving.

4 medium russet potatoes
canola oil nonstick cooking spray
salt
1 cup reduced-fat cheddar
    cheese

8 teaspoons Hormel Real Bacon
    Pieces
1 tablespoon snipped fresh
    chives
⅓ cup sour cream

1. Preheat oven to 400 degrees.
2. Bake the potatoes for 1 hour or until tender.
3. When potatoes have cooled enough so that you can handle them, make two lengthwise cuts through each potato, resulting in three ½- to ¾-inch slices. Discard the middle slices or save them for a separate dish of mashed potatoes. This will leave you with two potato skins per potato.
4. With a spoon, scoop some of the potato out of each skin, being sure to leave about ¼ inch of potato inside of the skin.
5. Pop oven temperature up to 450 degrees.
6. Spray the entire surface of each potato skin, inside and out, with a light coating of the canola oil spray.
7. Place the skins on a baking sheet, open side up, salt each one,

and then bake them for 12 to 15 minutes or until the edges begin to brown.

8. Spread about two tablespoons of cheese on each of the potato skins.

9. Sprinkle a teaspoon of bacon pieces on top of the cheese on each potato skin.

10. Bake the skins for another 2 to 4 minutes or until cheese is melted. Remove the skins from the oven and transfer them to a serving plate.

11. Combine the chives with the sour cream and serve in a small sauce cup in the center of the plate, with the skins arranged around the sour cream, like spokes on a wheel.

- SERVES 4 AS AN APPETIZER.

Nutrition Facts (per serving)

SERVING SIZE—3 PIECES   TOTAL SERVINGS—4

	LOW-FAT	ORIGINAL
CALORIES (APPROX.)	302	420
FAT (APPROX.)	5G	14G

• • • •

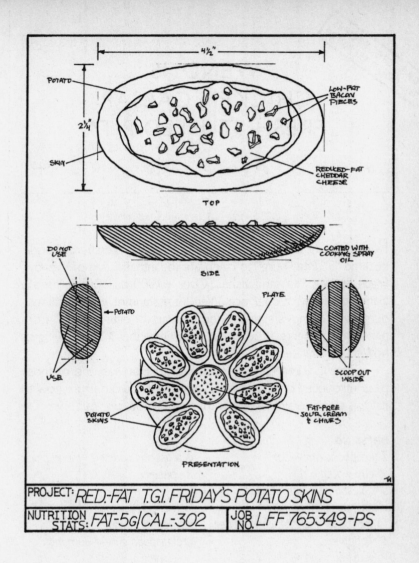

4½"

POTATO

2¼"

SKIN

LOW-FAT
BACON
PIECES

REDUCED-FAT
CHEDDAR
CHEESE

TOP

COATED WITH
COOKING SPRAY
OIL

SIDE

DO NOT
USE

←POTATO

USE

PLATE

SCOOP OUT
INSIDE

POTATO
SKINS

FAT-FREE
SOUR CREAM
& CHIVES

PRESENTATION

PROJECT: RED-FAT T.G.I. FRIDAY'S POTATO SKINS

NUTRITION STATS: FAT-5g/CAL.-302

JOB NO. LFF 765349-PS

WENDY'S CHICKEN CAESAR FRESH STUFFED PITA

☆   ✌   💣   🖊   ☯   ✂   ☞

Publicity stunt alert! For one day in 1997, St. Petersburg, Florida, became "St. Pitas-burg" to celebrate the introduction of Wendy's Fresh Stuffed Pita sandwiches. Over 40,000 balloons formed a giant pita sandwich on a local Wendy's restaurant, while local residents and Wendy's staff learned the "art of eating a pita" from pita eating experts. (I hear that next time, they'll be showing us how to drink water.)

The Chicken Caesar Fresh Stuffed Pita was one of those pitas introduced on that glorious day. See if you can figure how to eat this clone version, made with much less fat, on your own.

DRESSING

2 teaspoons arrowroot
½ cup water
3 tablespoons white vinegar
2 teaspoons lemon juice
¼ teaspoon finely minced red bell pepper
½ teaspoon salt
½ teaspoon granulated sugar
⅛ teaspoon garlic powder

⅛ teaspoon coarsely ground black pepper
dash dried parsley
dash dried oregano
dash dried thyme
1 tablespoon grated Romano cheese
1 tablespoon egg substitute

oil cooking spray
2 skinless chicken breast fillets
salt

ground black pepper
6 cups romaine lettuce, chopped
¼ cup red cabbage, shredded

¼ cup carrot, shredded
4 large pita breads

4 teaspoons shredded, fresh
Parmesan

1. Make the dressing by dissolving the arrowroot in the water. Heat the water in the microwave for 1 to 1½ minutes or until it begins to boil. Add the remaining ingredients except the Romano cheese and egg substitute, and let the mixture cool. When the mixture has reached room temperature, add the cheese and egg substitute. Cover and chill this dressing until it's thick.
2. Preheat a barbecue or indoor grill to medium heat. Spray a little oil cooking spray on each chicken breast. Salt and pepper the chicken, then grill it for 5 minutes per side or until done. Remove the chicken from the grill and dice it.
3. While chicken cooks, prepare the salad by combining the romaine lettuce, red cabbage, and shredded carrot in a large bowl and toss.
4. Prepare the sandwiches by first microwaving each pita for 20 seconds. Fold each pita in half like a taco, then fill them with 1 to 1½ cups of romaine salad each.
5. Add about ⅓ cup of diced chicken on top of the salad in the pita.
6. Pour about a tablespoon of dressing over each sandwich.
7. Sprinkle about a teaspoon of shredded fresh Parmesan on top of each sandwich, and serve.

- MAKES 4 SANDWICHES.

Nutrition Facts (per serving)
SERVING SIZE—1 SANDWICH   TOTAL SERVINGS—4

	LOW-FAT	ORIGINAL
CALORIES (APPROX.)	283	490
FAT (APPROX.)	5G	18G

• • • •

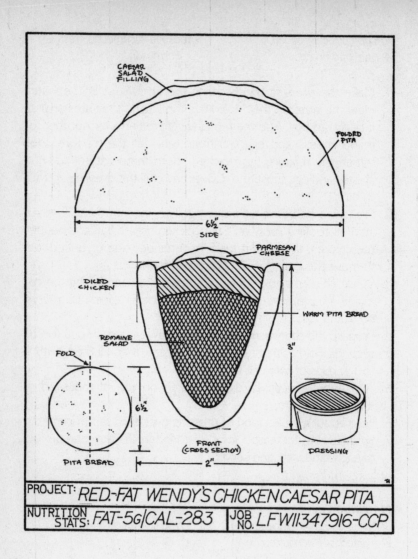

CAESAR SALAD FILLING

FOLDED PITA

6½"
SIDE

PARMESAN CHEESE

DICED CHICKEN

WARM PITA BREAD

ROMAINE SALAD

FOLD

3"

6½"

PITA BREAD

FRONT
(CROSS SECTION)

2"

DRESSING

PROJECT: RED.-FAT WENDY'S CHICKEN CAESAR PITA

NUTRITION STATS: FAT-5g/CAL.-283

JOB NO. LFW11347916-CCP

WENDY'S
CLASSIC GREEK
FRESH STUFFED PITA

☆ ✄ 💣 🖊 ⚫ ✂ ☞

Publicity stunt alert number two! In 1997, Wendy's announced its IPO—otherwise known as the Initial Pita Offering—on the floor of the New York Stock Exchange. Wendy's CEO Gordon Teter rang the bell to open the day of trading while Wendy's stock traders on the floor munched out on four varieties of the pita sandwiches, including this one, the Classic Greek Fresh Stuffed Pita.

For our low-fat clone, we'll save a gaggle of grams by making the dressing fat-free, and then we'll use low-fat feta cheese. Following this secret formula below, you can turn what is normally a 20-fat-gram sandwich into one that weighs in with only 2.5 grams.

FAT-FREE DRESSING

2 teaspoons arrowroot
½ cup water
3 tablespoons white vinegar
2 teaspoons lemon juice
¼ teaspoon finely minced red bell pepper
½ teaspoon salt
½ teaspoon granulated sugar
⅛ teaspoon garlic powder

⅛ teaspoon coarsely ground black pepper
dash dried parsley
dash dried oregano
dash dried thyme
1 tablespoon grated Romano cheese
1 tablespoon egg substitute

1 cup crumbled low-fat feta
  cheese
½ cup tomato, seeded and diced
¼ cup cucumber, thinly sliced and
  chopped

¼ cup red onion, diced
6 cups romaine lettuce, chopped
¼ cup red cabbage, shredded
¼ cup carrot, shredded
4 large pita breads

1. Make the dressing by dissolving the arrowroot in the water. Heat the water in the microwave for 1 to 1½ minutes or until it begins to boil. Add the remaining ingredients except the Romano cheese and egg substitute, and let the mixture cool. When the mixture has reached room temperature, add the cheese and egg substitute. Cover and chill until thick.

2. Make the Greek topping for the sandwich by combining the crumbled feta cheese, tomato, cucumber, and red onion in a small bowl.

3. Prepare the salad by combining the romaine lettuce, red cabbage, and carrot in a large bowl and toss.

4. Prepare the sandwiches by first microwaving each pita for 20 seconds. Fold each pita in half like a taco, then fill them with 1 to 1½ cups of romaine salad each.

5. Add ½ to ⅓ cup of the Greek topping to each sandwich.

6. Pour about a tablespoon of the dressing over each sandwich, and serve.

• MAKES 4 SANDWICHES.

Nutrition Facts (per serving)
SERVING SIZE—1 SANDWICH   TOTAL SERVINGS—4

	LOW-FAT	ORIGINAL
CALORIES (APPROX.)	240	440
FAT (APPROX.)	2.5G	20G

• • • •

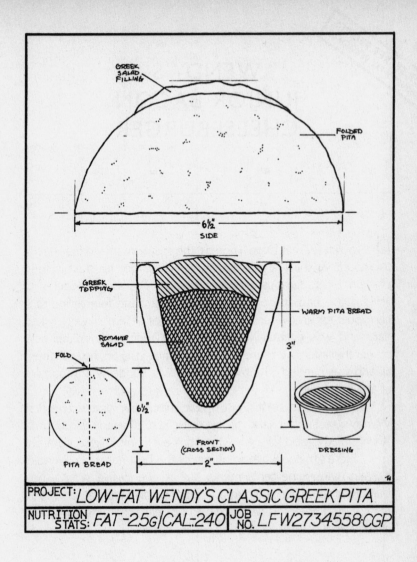

GREEK
SALAD
FILLING

FOLDED
PITA

6½"
SIDE

GREEK
TOPPING

WARM PITA BREAD

ROMAINE
SALAD

3"

FOLD

6½"

PITA BREAD

FRONT
(CROSS SECTION)

2"

DRESSING

PROJECT: *LOW-FAT WENDY'S CLASSIC GREEK PITA*

NUTRITION STATS: *FAT—2.5g/CAL—240*   JOB NO. *LFW2734558-CGP*

TOP SECRET RECIPES
REDUCED-FAT VERSION OF

WENDY'S JUNIOR BACON CHEESEBURGER

☆   ✂   💣   ✏   ⚫   ✄   ☞

Did you know that Dave Thomas, the spokesman and founder of the country's third-largest hamburger chain, got his start in fried chicken with a famous Kentucky colonel? That's right, kiddies! In 1962, Dave had an opportunity to turn around four failing KFC carryouts for an ownership stake in the lot of 'em. Dave worked hard and was eventually successful. He then parlayed his new ownership into four more KFC restaurants. In 1968, he sold them all and was handed $1.5 million. Dave was suddenly a millionaire at age thirty-five.

Not one to sit still, just a year later, Dave opened his first Wendy's restaurant, and today the chain is nearly 5000 units strong. Pretty good for a guy who didn't even finish high school, eh?

Here's my conversion of one of the best items on Wendy's bargain ninety-nine-cents menu, but at twenty-five grams (hey, that's four cents per fat gram!), it's just got too much fat, don't you think? Let's knock this one down to just eleven grams, using lean ground beef, fat-free mayo, and turkey bacon.

1 plain hamburger bun	½ tablespoon fat-free mayonnaise
⅛ pound super lean ground beef (7% fat)	1 slice fat-free American cheese
salt	2 strips turkey bacon
ground black pepper	1 lettuce leaf
	1 tomato slice

1. Brown the faces of the bun in a hot frying pan over medium heat. Keep the pan hot.
2. Form the ground beef into a square patty approximately 4 × 4 inches.
3. Cook the patty in the pan for 3 to 4 minutes per side or until done. Salt and pepper each side while cooking.
4. Spread the fat-free mayonnaise on the face of the top bun.
5. Place the cooked patty on the bottom bun.
6. Stack the cheese on the meat.
7. Place the bacon on the cheese.
8. Put the lettuce on next, then the tomato.
9. Top off the sandwich with the top bun. Microwave for 15 seconds on high to warm, if necessary.

- MAKES 1 SANDWICH.

Nutrition Facts *(per serving)*
SERVING SIZE—1 SANDWICH   TOTAL SERVINGS—1

	LOW-FAT	ORIGINAL
CALORIES (APPROX.)	310	430
FAT (APPROX.)	11G	25G

• • • •

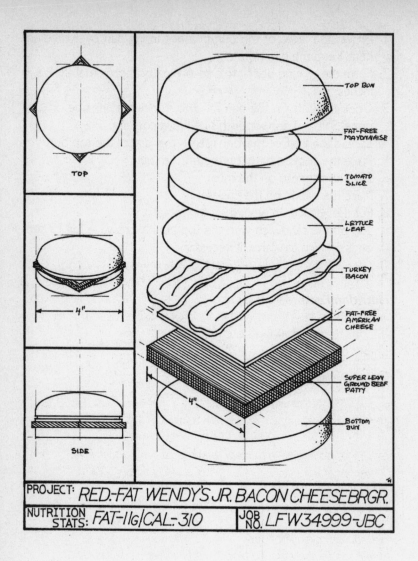

TOP

SIDE

4"

4"

TOP BUN

FAT-FREE MAYONNAISE

TOMATO SLICE

LETTUCE LEAF

TURKEY BACON

FAT-FREE AMERICAN CHEESE

SUPER LEAN GROUND BEEF PATTY

BOTTOM BUN

PROJECT: RED.-FAT WENDY'S JR. BACON CHEESEBRGR.

NUTRITION STATS: FAT-11g/CAL.-310

JOB NO. LFW34999-JBC

TOP SECRET RECIPES
REDUCED-FAT VERSION OF

WENDY'S
SPICY CHICKEN FILLET
SANDWICH

☆   ✌   💣   🖊   ☯   ✂   ☞

Wendy's kicked it up a notch in 1996 when the burger chain introduced the Spicy Chicken Fillet Sandwich. The deep-fried chicken fillet in the middle of this puppy is breaded with a secret coating containing just a bit of zing for those who like their food with some heat. It's not exactly the knock-your-socks-off kind of hot, but the spice gives the chicken a great flavor that's got customers coming back for more.

In this Top Secret Recipes reduced-fat conversion, you'll learn how to get that heat in the chicken, and then how to use a special baking technique that will give the cluck meat a breaded-and-fried consistency without too much oil.

⅓ cup Frank's Original Red Hot
    Pepper Sauce
⅔ cup water
1 cup all-purpose flour
2½ teaspoons salt
4 teaspoons cayenne pepper
1 teaspoon coarsely ground black
    pepper
1 teaspoon onion powder
½ teaspoon paprika

⅛ teaspoon garlic powder
2 skinless chicken breast
    fillets
oil cooking spray
8 teaspoons fat-free
    mayonnaise
4 plain hamburger buns
4 tomato slices
4 lettuce leaves

1. Preheat oven to 475 degrees.
2. Combine the pepper sauce and water in a small bowl.

3. Combine the flour, salt, cayenne pepper, black pepper, onion powder, paprika, and garlic powder in another shallow bowl.

4. Slice each of the breast fillets in half across the middle. Wrap each piece of chicken in plastic wrap and pound it with a mallet to about ¼ inch thick. If necessary, trim each breast fillet to help it fit on the bun.

5. Working with one slice of chicken at a time, coat each piece with the flour mixture, then dredge it in the diluted pepper sauce. Coat the chicken once again in the flour mixture, and set it aside until the rest of the chicken is breaded.

6. Line a large baking sheet with aluminum foil. Spray foil with a generous coat of oil cooking spray. Arrange all of the breaded chicken onto the sprayed foil. Spray a light coat of the oil spray over the entire surface of each slice of chicken.

7. Bake chicken for 8 to 12 minutes or until it begins to brown. Crank oven up to a high broil and broil for 3 to 5 minutes per side or until the surface begins to become crispy. (Be careful not to cook too long, or chicken may dry out.)

8. As chicken bakes, spread about 2 teaspoons of mayonnaise on the face of each of the inverted top buns.

9. Place a tomato slice onto the mayonnaise, and a leaf of lettuce on top of the tomato.

10. When the chicken is done, stack one piece onto each of the bottom buns.

11. Flip the top half of each sandwich onto the bottom half, and serve hot.

- MAKES 4 SANDWICHES.

Nutrition Facts (per serving)

SERVING SIZE—1 SANDWICH   TOTAL SERVINGS—4

	LOW-FAT	ORIGINAL
CALORIES (APPROX.)	380	410
FAT (APPROX.)	8G	15G

• • • •

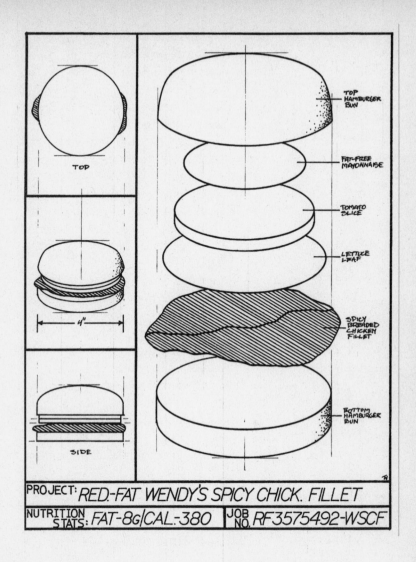

TOP

SIDE

4"

TOP HAMBURGER BUN

FAT-FREE MAYONNAISE

TOMATO SLICE

LETTUCE LEAF

SPICY BREADED CHICKEN FILLET

BOTTOM HAMBURGER BUN

PROJECT: *RED-FAT WENDY'S SPICY CHICK. FILLET*

NUTRITION STATS: *FAT-8g/CAL.-380*

JOB NO.: *RF3575492-WSCF*

TRADEMARKS

Applebee's and Low-Fat & Fabulous are registered trademarks of Applebee's International, Inc.

Bennigan's is a registered trademark of Metromedia Co.

California Pizza Kitchen is a registered trademark of California Pizza Kitchen, Inc.

Carl's Jr., Charbroiled Santa Fe Chicken Sandwich, and Ranch Crispy Chicken Sandwich are registered trademarks of Carl Karcher Enterprises, Inc.

Chevys and Fresh Mex are registered trademarks of Chevys, Inc.

Chili's is a registered trademark of Brinker International.

Entenmann's and Entenmann's Light are registered trademarks of Entenmann's, Inc.

Gardenburger is a registered trademark of Gardenburger, Inc.

Girl Scout Cookies is a registered trademark of Girl Scouts U.S.A.

Healthy Choice is a registered trademark of ConAgra, Inc.

Keebler and Pecan Sandies are registered trademarks of Keebler Company.

KFC is a registered trademark of Kentucky Fried Chicken Corporation.

Koo Koo Roo and Original Skinless Flame-Broiled Chicken are registered trademarks of Koo Koo Roo, Inc.

Little Debbie and Oatmeal Lights are registered trademarks of McKee Foods Corporation.

McDonald's, Egg McMuffin, and Arch Deluxe are registered trademarks of McDonald's Corporation.

Nabisco, Honey Maid Grahams, Oreo, SnackWell's, Apple Raisin Snack Bars, and Banana Snack Bars are registered trademarks of Nabisco, Inc.

Olive Garden is a registered trademark of Darden Restaurants, Inc.

Otis Spunkmeyer is a registered trademark of Otis Spunkmeyer, Inc.

Outback Steakhouse, Walkabout Soup, and Alice Springs Chicken are registered trademarks of Outback Steakhouse, Inc.

Panda Express is a registered trademark of Panda Management Company, Inc.

Planters, Fiddle Faddle, and Screaming Yellow Zonkers are registered trademarks of Planters, Inc.

Rainforest Cafe, Reggae Beat Seasoning, Rumble in the Jungle Turkey Pita, and Chicken Quartet are registered trademarks of Rainforest Cafe, Inc.

Seven Seas is a registered trademark of Kraft Foods, Inc.

Sonic Drive-In is a registered trademark of Sonic Drive-In Restaurants, Inc.

Taco Bell and Beef Burrito Supreme are registered trademarks of Taco Bell Corp.

T.G.I. Friday's is a registered trademark of T.G.I. Friday's, Inc.

Tootsie Roll is a registered trademark of Tootsie Roll Industries.

Wendy's, Chicken Caesar Fresh Stuffed Pita, and Classic Greek Fresh Stuffed Pita are registered trademarks of Wendy's International.

INDEX